BE CAREFUL WITH MUHAMMAD!

BE CAREFUL WITH MUHAMMAD!

The Salman Rushdie Affair

Shabbir Akhtar

Bellew Publishing
London

To those on the other side —
in the hope that they may understand
our pain.

First published in Great Britain in 1989 by
Bellew Publishing Company Ltd.,
7 Southampton Place,
London WC1A 2DR

Copyright © Shabbir Akhtar 1989

ISBN 0 947792 27 9

Phototypeset by Input Typesetting Ltd, London
Printed and bound in Great Britain by
Mackays of Chatham

Contents

Preface

An illiterate woman in Bradford went to see her teenage daughter's schoolteacher, who said to her: '*The Satanic Verses* is brilliant! In Britain we like to read great literature.' She remained silent and returned home. This book is an attempt to explain that inarticulate believer's anguish. If it achieves anything more, it will be a bonus.

I have written this book in difficult conditions. We were in the midst of the campaign against *The Satanic Verses*; and success was not in sight. But many people have, in widely different ways, helped me to survive:

Ishtiaq Ahmed, Naila Ahmed, Zamir Akhtar, Arfana Amin, Shahida Bano, Ib Bellew, David Caute, Kenneth Cragg, Courtney Gibson, Balbir Kaur, Fazlun Khalid, Rashid Mufti, Bhikhu Parekh, Andrew Robinson, Mohammed Saddique, Ziauddin Sardar, Ahmed Versi, and Riffat Yusuf, to mention but a few.

I also wish to thank Rehana Ahmed for cheerfully and accurately typing the manuscript with such dispatch; and, finally, someone very close to me who always reminds me that every human being has the right to fail.

SHABBIR AKHTAR
Bradford, August 1989

'Believers! Be resolute in the doing of justice,
as witnesses to God, even though it be
against your own souls, your parents or your
relatives, and whether it concerns the rich or
the poor. For in the eyes of God neither
wealth nor poverty carry any weight. Do not
follow your own desires and thereby pervert
the truth. Yet if you decide to act in bias and
prejudice, God is well aware of the things you
do.'

Koran, *The Women*, v. 135

NOTE It is customary for Muslim writers to
place the pious expression 'Peace be upon
him' after every mention of the name
Muhammad, especially in devotional
contexts. The author hopes that it does not
seem unduly irreverent to omit this
expression in a primarily argumentative work.

1 Be Careful with Muhammad!

1

'Say what you like about God—but be careful with Muhammad!' is an old slogan of Western caution about Islam, but one which we might well take seriously in the wake of the controversy surrounding the publication of Salman Rushdie's *The Satanic Verses*. The missionaries and other Christians who preached the Gospel in Islamic lands often found Muslims to be obstinate in their religious convictions and protective about their Prophet. While Muslims tended to accept some forms of satire or parody of the divine ways, they rarely tolerated insults to Muhammad and his family. Belief in God was common to Jews, Christians and Muslims. But endorsement of Muhammad's prophethood was the distinguishing feature of the Muslim outlook. It was the responsibility of Muslims, therefore, to guard the honour of *their* Prophet, the Arabian messenger who had brought them guidance from God.

Salman Rushdie's *The Satanic Verses* is seen by Muslims as a calculated attempt to vilify and slander the Prophet of Islam. Not only has Rushdie said what he pleased about God, he has also taken liberties with Muhammad. The reaction of the Muslim communities world-wide has been loud and clear. The only recent event to have triggered off Muslim emotion on a scale even remotely comparable to the Rushdie affair was the attempt to destroy the al-Aqsa mosque in Jerusalem two decades ago. It will not be our task here to recall all the many dimensions of the Rushdie saga that have crowded the world's headlines for many months. But it will be our task to see why so many Muslims have been willing to spill much more than merely ink over *The Satanic Verses*.

Muhammad ibn Abdullah is, on every score of influence and achievement, a decisive figure in the history of theistic religion. His contribution to the human quest for the holy cannot be reasonably denied. Even so, someone might wonder, why the caution? Why should one be careful with Muhammad? Is he any different from any other historical figure? After all, Moses and Jesus also have vast ideological legacies but the same demand for caution, especially these days, seems unnecessary.

Moses, Jesus and Muhammad are all seminal figures in the history of Western theism. But Muslims jealously guard the reputation of their Prophet in a manner that looks odd even to Jews and Christians, let alone to secularists and rejectors. In the Jewish case, disrespect towards Moses and other Hebrew prophets is tolerated. In fact, blasphemy is restricted to cursing the Lord; insulting Moses is, strictly speaking, not blasphemous: 'Say what you like about Moses—but be careful with God.' As for Jesus, wanton attacks on his personality and the associated Christian convictions have been commonplace in recent decades in secular Western societies. In general, Christians have tolerated these affronts; the character assassination of Jesus has been carried out with impunity.

Muhammad is unique in the respect and honour afforded him by his followers. Though not regarded as divine, Muhammad is held in the highest possible esteem. No pictorial representations are allowed; mention of his name warrants, among the pious, the invocation of divine blessing on him, his family and companions. His wives are seen as the mothers of the faithful. Every detail of his biography has been preserved and countless millions seek to imitate him daily in every aspect of their lives.

The reason for the caution, then, is what may be called 'the posthumous authority of Muhammad'. The influence of the Arabian Prophet on the lives of millions, through the patterns of his biography daily imitated, is without parallel in the whole of history, religious or secular. The imitation of Muhammad is, unlike the imitation of Christ, an accepted obligation, a routine occurrence. It is the ideal not only for the saints—but for all Muslims, from the beggars in the slums of India to the spectacularly wealthy sheikhs of Saudi Arabia, from the illiterate peasants of Pakistan to the erudite scholars of al-Azhar, from the village women of the Third World to the sophisticates of Western female society.

Muhammad is dead. But he is dead only in the least significant sense. For he is ideologically alive — and well. The Rushdie affair has demonstrated the extent of Muslim enthusiasm about their messenger and, in doing so, the quality of their allegiance to the ideals he preached. The fact is that the Prophet of Islam is resurrected daily in what must be the greatest triumph over the limitations of physical extinction. It is therefore unsurprising that any attempt to prostitute his reputation should have met with such resolute and uncompromising opposition.

2

In chapter 33 (verse 21), the Koran describes the life of Muhammad as 'a beautiful exemplar' (*uswatan hasanah*). Elsewhere in the sacred volume, the Prophet is also extolled as the model of righteousness, the perfect individual. His actions and ambitions are held to be worthy of our close scrutiny and imitation. Naturally, for the Muslim conscience the imitation of the Prophet becomes a morally excellent action. Conversely, any attack on this holy pattern is already an attack on a Muslim's own professed ideals.

It is in this context that we need to give a brief summary of the contents of *The Satanic Verses* and offer concisely a Muslim rejoinder. The brevity of these introductory remarks is not intended to imply any undue dogmatism or foreclosing of issues. All of the worries set out here will be carried forward into several subsequent chapters; this account should be read as foreshadowing the fuller ones that follow.

The plot of *The Satanic Verses*, in so far as it is intelligible, is centred around the lives of two ageing Indian actors, Gibreel Farishta (Gabriel the Angel) and Saladin Chamcha (Saladin 'the Yes man'). Miraculously, they survive the fall when a plane is blown up in a terrorist attack. Upon descent, they turn into fantastic embodiments of good and evil, with Chamcha, an Anglophile, representing evil. True to their names, Chamcha grows horns and begins to resemble the

Devil while his angelic companion acquires a halo. Though Chamcha is humiliated as a beast and betrayed by his companions, he is eventually redeemed by re-adopting his Eastern identity. Gibreel, by contrast, loses his mind, fails as a human being, and eventually commits suicide.

The story of their lives is inextricably linked to and redefined in terms of a background narrative about the Prophet Mahound who lives in the hedonistic metropolis of Jahilia (literally, ignorance)—the pre-Islamic name for Mecca. Now Mahound was, as Rushdie explains in the book, a derogatory name for the Prophet Muhammad, used in medieval Christendom. More precisely, Mahound was, in Christian mythology, an evil personality who joined forces with the Devil and King Herod. Mahound believes that he is the recipient of divine revelations which authorise him to preach and propagate a new monotheistic religion. According to Rushdie, Mahound, a 'businessman-turned-prophet' is, in an attempt to attract more followers, ready to entertain the pagan proposal that three Meccan goddesses share divine status with the supreme being, Allah. At first, Mahound believes that the proposal is divinely inspired; afterwards he realises that the Devil interfered in his reception of the divine message. Though Mahound decides to eradicate from his holy book these 'satanic verses'—from which Rushdie's novel takes its title— Mahound's book is in general a value-blind collection in which good is routinely confused with evil, divine with diabolic.

The two chapters 'Mahound' and 'Return to Jahilia', containing Gibreel's coherent dreams, are in effect Rushdie's attempt to rewrite chronologically the history of early Islam. Taken together, along with some subsidiary material in other chapters, these sections of the book proffer an alternative biography of Muhammad, his wives and companions.

Someone might immediately query the assumption that dream sequences in a novel can reasonably be interpreted to be an alternative historical account. But, as the Hindu writer Bhikhu Parekh has so ably shown (*New Statesman & Society*, 23 March 1989), the events and characters in *The Satanic Verses* bear so striking a resemblance to actual events and characters in Islamic history that one has grounds to doubt its status as merely fictional. Muhammad was called Mahound by Western polemicists; the episode of the satanic verses is, according to many learned authorities in Islam, an authentic one in the history of the revelation of the Arabic Koran; Rushdie's Mahound has wives and companions who bear names identical to the names of Muhammad's wives and companions. Rushdie does not explore, in a fictional context, the religious mind or religious attitudes in general. He explores the Muslim mind—the 'Muhammadan' mind. The characters in *The Satanic Verses* are real historical personalities of the Islamic tradition—redefined, re-assessed, their motives and actions radically if imaginatively reinterpreted. That is why it is fair to note, as Gerald Priestland does (*Sunday Times*, 6 November 1988), that Rushdie's book is indeed 'a parody of the prophet Muhammad', and, therefore, one should add, of Islam and the derivative Islamic tradition.

The details of the parody must await the next chapter. Only a few comments are in order here. The title itself does not reflect the dominant theme or content; the name Mahound is chosen without adequate literary reason. The character assassination of the Arabian Prophet is here carried out with a precision and ferocity that would shock any decent human being, let alone a Muslim. There are serious allegations: Muhammad is an unscrupulous politician—'a smart bastard' in Rushdie's phrase—whose enemies, particularly ideological ones, are the victims of a ruthless anger discrepant with his official professions of mercy; the book he claims to bring from God is really just a confused catalogue of trivial rules about sexual activity and excretion. Muhammad, according to *The Satanic Verses*, was a debauched sensualist with 'God's permission to fuck as many women as he pleased'; his household is portrayed in pornographic scenes in a brothel incongruously called 'The Veil'—the symbol of female modesty and chastity in the Islamic ethical outlook.

A man who brought a book that directly inspired a major world civilisation is here portrayed as an insincere impostor with purely political ambitions. The revered Prophet of an established and ancient faith re-emerges as a man motivated

5

by purely and irredeemably evil impulses. Muslim anger and resentment are easy to understand.

Had the voice of mockery in *The Satanic Verses* been even slightly more subdued, there would have been grounds for restraint and forbearance. But an authentic Muslim is bound to feel intolerably outraged by the book's claims, for Rushdie writes with all the knowledge of an insider. This is not to deny his right to explore, in fiction, the great parameters of life, sexuality, mortality and the existence (or non-existence) of deity. But Muslims must and do take issue with his choice of idiom and the temper it serves. His treatment is uniformly supercilious and dismissive; his reservations are shallow, playful, predictable, unoriginal. One looks in vain in his unprincipled prose for the reverent yet iconoclastic doubt which might set the agenda for the Islamic Enlightenment. There is nothing in *The Satanic Verses* which helps to bring Islam into a fruitful confrontation with modernity, nothing that brings it into thoughtful contact with contemporary secularity and ideological pluralism. Rushdie's scepticism fails to teach the ignorant, disturb the orthodox, agitate and educate the indifferent. Sceptics there have been and always will be. What matters is the quality and integrity of their reservations.

Let me introduce an autobiographical note here. Ever since the publication of *The Satanic Verses* in September 1988, my name has been associated with the campaign for its withdrawal. Though there are pressures of professional diplomacy in public contexts, I wish to make my position perfectly clear. I believe that *The Satanic Verses* is a calculated attempt to vilify and slander Muhammad. It is my conviction that while freedoms of belief, expression, conscience, and dissent are rightly valued in a liberal democratic society, it is immoral to defend, in the name of these freedoms, wanton attacks on established religious (and indeed humanist) traditions. There is all the difference in the world between sound historical criticism that is legitimate and ought to be taken seriously, on the one hand, and scurrilous imaginative writing which should be resolutely rejected and withdrawn from public circulation.

What matters here is not simply that Rushdie has falsified

established historical records or even that he has written a satire about things sacred. There are wider issues too which hinge on the fact that we live in a society that is often described as multi-racial (or rather, multi-cultural, for there is only one race, the human race). It is unwise for us, in such a context, casually to allow our idolatry of art to obscure issues of great social and political concern. One would think that, in a plural democracy, we should all generate respect rather than hatred for opposed yet conscientiously held convictions. To be sure, there will be conflicts; and writers have the right to identify and condemn evil and injustice wherever they find them without being unduly shackled by fear of giving offence. But these frictions and differences are containable in a mature democracy so long as we do not tolerate, let alone encourage, a form of ridicule that breeds resentment to the point of frustration and hence personal and social dislocation. It can never be right to defend, in the name of liberalism, works that demean and humiliate human nature and tradition in any of their established forms. Militant evil has enough sponsors already without liberal society lending another helping hand.

3

The question of Rushdie is inseparable from the question of Muhammad and his faith. The Prophet has been the target of Western animus periodically for one-and-a-half millennia. The current debate has, at this late hour, virtually nothing to do with Rushdie or his book, let alone with freedom of speech. For these latter debates are containable and indeed resolvable given the modesty of the Muslim demand and the capacity of Western governments to fulfil it. The Rushdie affair retains its momentum largely because of the incidence of deep psychic tensions within a Western conscience confronting an authentically Islamic temper. Part of the concern here is fuelled by the contemporary fear, in itself absurdly unrealistic, that Muslim immigrant populations want to build a theocracy in the heart of a European country. But, more plausibly, for complex historical reasons, Islam has always

been a threatening presence on and around Western fron-
tiers—and not merely on account of its geographical proxim-
ity. Indeed the threat has been to the whole of 'the West'
in the ideological (rather than geographical) sense of the
civilisation created, through world-wide colonial exploitation,
by the peoples of Europe. It is not surprising that the faith
of the Arabian Prophet is increasingly a major variable in the
ideological calculations of Christian missionaries and Western
apologists.

The parody of Muhammad and the Muslim tradition in *The
Satanic Verses* has clear echoes of the worst brand of orientalist sentiment for which the term 'prejudice' is decidedly lenient. Even if we leave aside the evil and unjust polemic of a
Dante in the Middle Ages, there is plenty of animus in works
published in the heyday of Western Christian imperialism.
Washington Irving's *Mahomet and His Successors* has, on its
title page, an imaginary painting of the Prophet with a sword
in one hand and a Koran in the other. His nineteenth-century
contemporary Sir William Muir is more explicit: 'The sword
of Mahomet, and the Coran are the most fatal enemies of
civilization, liberty and truth which the world has yet known.'

Little has changed over the centuries. Though some recent
academic scholarship has moved in the direction of objectivity
and imaginative sympathy, there has been no substantial shift
in opinion. As for the popular mind, the old prejudices certainly prevail. Barbaric, fanatical, out-dated, exotic, oppressive, sensual—all are contemporary Western descriptions of
Islam. Predictably the monotheism of Muhammad emerges
as the natural habitat of all the base passions—extravagant
sensuality, bloodthirstiness and fanaticism. Islam is the lower
unbridled nature of man, motivated by impulses which Christianity and civilisation together tame and control. Even the
sacred personalities of the Islamic tradition, including
Muhammad, are seen as fanatical and irredeemably evil, their
humanity overwhelmed by their lust for power.

There is a great deal of popular fiction and journalism to
perpetuate these and related assessments. Novels such as
Leon Uris's *Haj*, social critiques such as John Laffin's *The
Dagger of Islam*, travelogues such as V. S. Naipaul's *Among*

the Believers, films such as *Harem* and *Strike Force*—all convey the same picture of an intolerant and cruel faith whose votaries cling to bygone certainties. Nor are these portraits of Islam in serious conflict with Western academic scholarship. On the contrary, there is a whole host of disciplines, engaging countless 'experts', all united in their biased opinion of Islam. This negative image of Muslims and their faith is perpetuated with a consistency and vigour that makes at least one conspiracy theory appear close to the mark.

There are, of course, many grounds for the sustained Western animus against Islam. For one thing Islam was originally and has remained, for the Western Christian conscience, a religious puzzle. Why Muhammad and the Koran after Christ had walked among men as God incarnate and proffered ultimate salvation? Muslims, with much reason, regard Islam as the culmination of the Hebrew style of religiosity with Christianity as essentially an aberration. At any rate, the very existence of Islam in the world implies that the Judaeo-Christian faith complex does not exhaust the Western monotheistic tradition.

The problem of Islam has always been much more than merely 'religious'—if only because Muslims have always seen Islam as a unified enterprise of faith and power. Christians could hardly ignore the political potential of a religious ideology that has to its credit the fastest permanent conquest of recorded military history. To the medieval mind, nothing could explain the phenomenal success of the new faith other than as the work of the Devil. In later centuries the ambitions of Islamic imperialism continued to exercise Western apologists, who were themselves no strangers to that impulse.

Western apologists have always wanted to believe that Islam is an inferior and unoriginal faith and have always had difficulty in believing it. That Muhammad was an insincere impostor—'a smart bastard' as Rushdie would say—has always been hard to reconcile with his manifest achievements as a religious reformer. Islamic civilisation, based on a religiously sanctioned respect for literacy and scholarship, has since its inception remained a serious intellectual rival to the Christian outlook. Indeed Islam itself has been a great temptation to Christian believers; the rate of conversion from Christianity to Islam is the highest of any inter-faith movements, often attracting highly distinguished individuals.

4

Under the impact of increased tensions in the Muslim world in the last two decades there has been an attempt, quite deliberate and perhaps even co-ordinated, to construct an influential stereotype of contemporary 'fundamentalist' Islam. It is a stereotype that feeds on indelible images of apparently motiveless malice and terror. Hardly a day passes without some report of political violence in Iran, Lebanon, and Israel's Occupied Territories. And it is almost always fundamentalist Islam, according to the newscasters, that is agitating the Muslim masses.

Contemporary Western attitudes towards militant Islam are well reflected in the titles of recent books, *The Dagger of Islam*, *Sacred Rage*, *The Holy Killers of Islam*, and television documentaries, 'The Sword of Islam', 'The Fire of Islam', to mention but a few. It is rare that one comes across a widely available work whose author resists the temptation to sensationalism and opts for modest titles or sub-titles. Everywhere violent language like 'terror', 'rage', 'dagger', spices the title and triggers off reactions, variously, of withdrawal, anger, fear and contempt by readers located firmly within the Western constituency, in virtue of geography as well as of ideology and prejudice. It is revealing that many libraries innocently stock books on fundamentalist Islam under 'War and Terrorism'.

Where partisan political passion, whether for Islam or against it, is so firmly linked to scholarship, objectivity is hard to come by. Yet objectivity is something we desperately need. In their discussions of Islamic fundamentalism, both Muslims and their opponents need to re-assess emotive terminology and the negative images it conveys. For the choice of vocabulary is politically consequential. Part of the task here is to rescue terms such as 'militant Islam' and 'religious fundamentalism' from the disrepute into which they have fallen. It is all too easy and tempting to misuse these words. To call a movement 'fundamentalist' is, with many writers, already to discredit it. It is high time that we questioned the assumption prevalent in both academic and popular contexts, that fundamentalist options in religion necessarily lack intellectual credentials.

The insistence on a proper terminology is part of the larger concern to question stereotypical assessments. The dominant view of Islam among unsympathetic Christian and Marxist thinkers is that Islam is essentially a false religion with dangerous political potential. It is not surprising that their accounts employ a loaded terminology which betrays not only misunderstandings but often deliberate misrepresentations of the themes under discussion.

Take, for example, the old myth of Islam as an anti-intellectualist creed. Rushdie revives the view that the Koran radically vetoes scholarship, for it already contains all of it. 'Burn the books and trust the Book!' Rushdie's Imam, who has set his face against progress and knowledge, becomes the perfect Muslim. Yet the view is clearly laughable. For the scripture of Islam can claim the unique privilege of having directly inspired a major world civilisation based on a religiously sanctioned respect for literacy and learning. The early Muslims developed a great rational philosophical tradition which was itself part of the inspiration for both the Renaissance and the European Enlightenment. That Rushdie should choose to be a *literary* terrorist is itself a fitting tribute to the intelligent earnestness of Islam as a faith of the pen.

Islam is an influential and suggestive view of the world and of our place in it. Whether coherent or not, whether true or false, it has guided, and continues to guide, the lives of millions in a universal political constituency. Like any major ideology, it is a powerful vision with ambiguous potentialities— producing both moral greatness and enlightenment as well as appalling obscurantism and restriction of human sympathies. On every score, it deserves to be understood and properly assessed.

11

5

Muhammad is easily the most maligned religious personality in the whole of history. But he is also, I would argue, the most influential. Indeed the Rushdie affair is a conclusive confirmation of the extent of his posthumous authority for Muslims.

'Be careful with Muhammad', runs the cautionary maxim. It is as well to heed it. In 1924 a Hindu religionist in Lahore ignored the advice and published his iconoclastic *Rangila Rasul* ('The Merry Messenger' or 'The Playboy Prophet'). He insisted that Muhammad was a libertine whose religion was fit only for villains and impostors. The author was murdered by a Muslim; and the Muslim was hanged by the British authorities in India. One certainly had to be careful with Muhammad.

The life of the Arabian Prophet is of great interest to many thinkers and historians, whether Muslim, Jewish, Hindu or secular. It is also valid territory for imaginative reconstruction; after all even historical events are the subject of speculation and controversial interpretation. But neither historical nor fictional exploration of his biography can, with impunity, lapse into abuse and slander. Rushdie relishes scandalous suggestion and pejorative language. His account is uniformly self-indulgent, calculated to shock and humiliate Muslim sensibilities. It is unwise to ignore the role of provocation and polemic in exciting hatred and anger to the point of physical confrontation. In *The Satanic Verses*, Rushdie is handling the ultimate love and passion of millions. If one handles precious things, one does well to handle them with care.

2   Art or Literary Terrorism?

1

'The way in which art changes society', said Salman Rushdie in an interview in the autumn of 1988, 'is never in a broad sweep . . . —you write a book and governments fall—that never happens.' Doesn't it?

There are works of the pen—admittedly not novels—which topple dynasties. The Bible, the Koran, and *Das Kapital* are all books which have, in their different ways, undermined entire power structures that have resisted their revolutionary proposals. And in Rushdie's novel Mahound wrote a book and many governments—in fact two whole empires—fell. The pen can be mightier than the sword not least when its ink is used to praise it.

Let us turn now directly to Rushdie's novel. *The Satanic Verses* is, on every score of influence and publicity, a work which assures Rushdie a place in literary history and, according to Michael Foot, an honourable place in general history. In this chapter I shall review the book, examine its salient themes, and set down, rather starkly, the central objections that a Muslim conscience must necessarily raise.

I should say to begin with that Muslim critics of the work have been accused of taking the allegedly offending material out of context and throwing it about as, in Bhikhu Parekh's apt phrase, 'polemical hand grenades'. (*New Statesman and Society*, 23 March 1989). That many Muslim leaders have not read the whole book is true enough. But those who classify themselves as critics certainly have. To discuss some selected pieces out of a lengthy work is not in itself tantamount to ignoring the total context. A fair critic needs to be aware of the overall context and make clear its connection or signifi- cantly its lack of connection with the selected passages. That will be my procedure in the coming pages.

13

2

The Satanic Verses opens with a terrorist bomb that blows its two central characters out of the jumbo jet carrying them from Bombay to London (p.2). Gibreel Farishta and Saladin Chamcha—'us wogs' in Rushdie's phrase (p.51)—survive to represent a symbolic angel and devil respectively. Gibreel Farishta, an Indian film star, identified by some readers with the hugely popular real-life movie idol Amitabh Bachchan, is running away from his obligations in Bombay. He is forty when the story begins and very upset about his declining career. In the past Gibreel has often played Hindu deities in the Indian cinema. His illness creates, credibly, a national crisis and elicits even Rajiv Gandhi's sympathies (p.28).

Our other protagonist, Saladin Chamcha, is a middle-class Anglophile who wants to return to London after a theatrical season in India, during which his identity as a proper English gentleman has become difficult to sustain. As the son of a wealthy businessman, Saladin had the means to migrate to England early on in life. He found work as an actor and eventually as a dubber on commercials (p.60). Like his rich father, Saladin is thoroughly secular in his outlook (pp.43, 531). After falling from the aeroplane Saladin has acquired horns and hooves.

The narrative, in so far as it is coherent and intelligible, proceeds through a system of flashbacks on a variety of levels. For our purposes here, it is Gibreel's dream sequences in chapters 2 and 6 that need to be carefully examined. In them, the interaction between the good and the evil characters is defined and fleshed out in terms of a background story of Rushdie's Prophet, Mahound, who founds a new religion in the city of Jahilia—the pre-Islamic name for Islam's holy city. Chapters 2 and 6 together offer, in Muslim eyes, a crude caricature of the classic biography of Muhammad. Rushdie, through Gibreel's serial dreaming, offers an alternative account of the Prophet's activities in Mecca and, after the migration (*hijra*), in Medina. Parts of Chapter 6 supplement this narrative as Rushdie discusses the varied roles of God, Satan and the archangel Gabriel. The chapters 4 and 8 entitled 'Ayesha' and 'The Parting of the Arabian Sea' deal with a superstitious peasant girl in Rushdie's India who plans a pilgrimage, through the Arabian Sea, to Mecca. Given that Ayesha was, in real life, the Arabian Prophet's young wife and that a character by the same name appears in a brothel scene set in Muhammad's Mecca (pp.384 ff.) we cannot assume that these two chapters are irrelevant to Muslim reservations about the novel.

3

Several sections of the book are set in modern London. Though it will not be our task to examine these in detail, a few general comments are necessary to establish their relationship to the allegedly offensive material. Rushdie explores the difficulties of life in a multi-ethnic Western city, the meaning of migration, the dislocation both physical and psychological that the act of travelling entails. How do men and women cope with migration? (How did Mahound cope with his migration—*hijra*—from Mecca to Medina?)

In a sense *The Satanic Verses* is a tale of three cities— London, Bombay, and Jahilia. Indeed the three places are, says Rushdie in an interview reprinted in the *Bookseller* (Autumn 1988), 'really the same place'. And, accordingly, Rushdie writes as if they were. On one level, this simply means that the story of Mahound is told in a modern idiom— a mixture of journalese and irreverent Bombay diction. The whole ethos of Jahilia is distinctly Indian (as opposed to Arabian) with countless idioms, including swear-words, whose insinuations are lost upon Western readers. On the face of it, this makes *The Satanic Verses* seem peculiar and unconvincing.

But there is a much more powerful strain on credibility and it is one that relates directly to the larger question of the coherence of the 'magical realist' method in general. Is it indeed a coherent assumption that cities as historically and geographically diverse as Bombay, London and Jahilia are really the same place? For even places made contemporary by history may fail to be contemporary in ethos. And how much more must they fail in this respect if they also fail to be contemporary in time? If Bombay and London, in the same century, have little in common, neither Bombay nor London is likely to have much that is significantly in common with a seventh-century Arabian metropolis.

This is not to deny sympathy with the aim behind the assumption; it is to question its coherence and validity. The transference of an incident—its leading out, as it were—from one century indifferently to another—may be meant to illustrate the timelessness of moral norm and the human actions it shapes. Jahilia for Muslims, like Babylon for Christians, is a symbol of an irreligious and corrupt urban environment. How different then is Mahound's Jahilia from our Bombay? Isn't the human condition much the same in all places at all times? The answer is, of course, both in the affirmative and in the negative. In one sense, all the events in the world, in all places and at all times, are the same. Why? All the things we do, whether they unite us or divide us, are bound to unite us because all the actors are human. Even where there is rivalry in a game the players are united because the game they play is the same. In the human game, there is perversity, weakness, failure and sometimes triumph, whether the players be in London, Bombay, Jahilia or indeed anywhere else. But it is surely questionable whether or not one can meaningfully explore, beyond a certain point, our modern predicament in terms of seventh-century settings. It is a remarkable irony that Muslims eager to interpret the Koran for the benefit of modern audiences are frequently reminded that its ancient context renders it irrelevant to the twentieth century and its dilemmas.

This is not meant to be a conclusive objection to the method of *The Satanic Verses*. Attempts to explore, in fiction, the notion of cultural displacement do not easily succeed. And Rushdie does manage to convey something of the sense of guilt and creative doubt such displacement causes for the immigrant in general. The return from exile, the return to faith is not simply a once-and-for-all event in the past; it is part of a continuous present which renews and sustains a hybrid identity combining the past and the present.

Having said this, it is also worth saying that many parts of *The Satanic Verses* defy comprehension and tire even the sympathetic reader. Of course, there can be integrity in a fictional style mixing fantasy and unreality with truth and fact. And it is also sometimes necessary to educate contemporary sensibility by an appeal to the past. But the strains both on credibility and coherence are massive. *The Satanic Verses* visibly buckles under the pressure; and Rushdie does little to alleviate it. On the contrary, he is often self-indulgent, caring little for the reader puzzled by the complexity or incoherence—whichever sounds better—in some of the passages. There is nothing wrong, in principle, in the attempt to explore the relationship between an uprooted modern religious sensibility and the sacred record on which it feeds. But the obligation to maintain intelligibility (if not reverence) is surely paramount.

4

Rushdie has a fine insight into the deep, almost unjust, possessive love Indian mothers experience for their sons. Gibreel's mother lovingly refers to her dreamer son as both an angel and a devil. How revealing is this hint about the value-blindness of a mother's love! But equally, how unhelpful an implication it is on the metaphysical level. For devils are not angels; and good is not evil. Gibreel interiorises his mother's love and swallows with it, so to speak, the ambiguity of its motivation. In the process he becomes confused about his own identity.

The confusion of the sacred and the profane, the good and the evil, allegedly revealed truth and purely human truth, supplies the central metaphysical theme of the novel. Both the internal ambiguity in each of these categories and their dependence on each other interest Rushdie. Is Gibreel Farishta really an angel? Or is he insane? What is the true nature of good? If Gibreel's opposite number, Saladin Chamcha, appears to be the Devil, does that imply a *radical* increase in his capacity for evil? How much more evil is Chamcha than Gibreel or, for that matter, than you and I?

Rushdie takes the incident of 'the satanic verses' from early Islamic history in order to give dramatic form to the central, rather abstract, metaphysical theme of his work. Before we turn to an examination of that incident, it is worth noting Rushdie's own professed aims and assessing how far he succeeds. In a pre-publication interview, Rushdie remarked that in *The Satanic Verses* he 'wanted to work out some kind of ethic of impurity'. He went on to say that his Islam was 'not at all the pure faith of a Pakistani Muslim'. Rushdie's brand of Islam had been 'infiltrated by Hinduism, Sikhism, Christianity and other beliefs' one finds in a cosmopolitan multi-faith society such as India. His comment is interesting in the light of the Bradford Pakistani Muslims' decision to burn his book in January 1989, which could be seen as an attempt to avoid any contamination of their faithful heritage. Rushdie has his reasons for opposing the purists: 'Most of our problems begin when people try to define the world in terms of a stark opposition between good and evil, or in terms of racial or national purity.' (*Bookseller*).

This is certainly a salutary reminder. But surely it cannot be an apologia for deliberately making things impure. There are two separate issues here: one is the purity and integrity of an ideal (such as Islam or humanism). The other is the purity of those who espouse it. The fact that we all fail to live up to our professed ideals—a part of the failings of our common humanity—is not a reason for diluting the ideal. The fact that each of us, Muslim or non-Muslim, is a mixture of good and evil impulses, does not by itself imply that the metaphysical distinction between good and evil is somehow only relative rather than absolute.

I labour this point because the dispute is over the issue of the integrity of the distinction between good and evil. Theists believe that the created world is endowed with this integrity by God's own decree or fiat. The plot of Rushdie's novel involves a radical questioning both of that integrity and of the allegedly divine procedure for maintaining it in the real world. It questions both by noting the failure of men and women to attain either complete evil or complete good in their lives. Put in this way, one can see that the argument is bound to be invalid. Our failure to attain either pure good or pure evil in our lives does not imply that there is no distinction between good and evil. As for Rushdie's obscure metaphysical claim that good and evil have a common origin, it is difficult even to grasp its meaning. In any case, having a common origin need not entail any subsequent lack of distinction: the fact that men and women have a common origin in their mother's wombs does not entail that there is no real distinction between the sexes.

5

Rushdie takes the incident of 'the satanic verses' as a basis for exploring the temptation to opportunism and compromise in the advocacy of religious creed. According to two early learned authorities, ibn Sa'd and a Persian historian at Tabari, Satan successfully interfered in the reception of the revealed text on one occasion. During the revelation of the 53rd chapter, the divinely revealed verses 19 and 20 ('Have you considered al-Lat and al-'Uzza and Manat, the third, the other?') were followed by two additional verses inspired by the Devil: 'These are the exalted birds whose intercession is to be desired.' Since the three idols mentioned were regarded as deities by the pagan Meccans—in fact as daughters of the supreme being, Allah—these satanic verses were wrongly thought to authorise their claim to divinity. So Muhammad's God had accepted the gods of the Meccans as having equal divine status: the audience, both Muslim and pagan, fell down in prostration, united for once. The Prophet was pleased to note a dramatic increase in the number of adherents to the new faith. A subsequent revelation, however, in chapter 17 (vv. 73–5) indicates that the passages warranting acceptance of the pagan goddesses were inspired by Satan. Accordingly, the satanic contribution was removed from the sacred corpus; and the resulting canon has, from the earliest times, enjoyed universal currency.

The incident has been disputed by many Muslims both in the past and the present and even by one or two non-Muslims, most notably the great Italian Islamicist Caetani. But the

Koran itself, notably in chapter 22 (v. 52) recognises the risks and liabilities of divine revelation. Consequently, recitations of the Koran, both in public and in private, are always prefaced by a declaration seeking divine immunity from diabolic influence.

Though many Muslims reject its authenticity, the incident of the satanic verses is actually a tribute both to the scrupulous honesty of a Muslim tradition that recorded such a potentially damaging event and also to the integrity and sincerity of Muhammad as God's spokesman. For elsewhere, in recognition of Muhammad's illiteracy and lack of mental independence in the face of divine revelation, the Koran counsels him to recite exactly what the angel shows him. According to Islamic orthodoxy, rightly or wrongly, Muhammad's role in the reception of the revelation was that of a robot. His own faculties were suspended, there being no conscious authorship. In the case of the controversial chapter 53, the Prophet was following the Koran's own advice about his role in the human reception of the divine word.

According to Rushdie (pp.112–24), the satanic revelation is self-induced by Mahound in order to please his arch-enemy, the disbelieving Abu Simbal—or historically, Abu Sufyan, identifiable on account of Rushdie's reference to his wife Hind. Mahound's own disciples, Khalid, Hamza, Salman, and Bilal are disappointed by the concessions implied in 'the satanic verses'. Rushdie insinuates that the Abyssinian slave Bilal, who converted to Islam, was a more committed monotheist than Mahound. Indeed Abu Simbal's passionate spouse, Hind, emerges as more uncompromising in her idolatry than Mahound in his Islam. Impressed by the severity of the pagan conscience, Mahound decides to reject his earlier compromise and invents a new version compatible with his strict Islamic monotheism. Rushdie's Prophet Mahound emerges, then, as an insincere pragmatist willing to sacrifice his principles to attract followers.

Rushdie takes an arguably real incident in the history of the revelation of the Arabic Koran and makes it into the basis of sweeping and gratuitous accusations. The sacred scripture of Islam is reduced to a value-blind catalogue of trivial rules about 'every damn thing' (p.363) issued by a God who 'sounded so much like a businessman' (p.364). The recipient of the revelations was 'no angel, you understand' (p.366), the occasions of the revelations well timed to suit his personal wishes and the political requirements of his situation (p.364).

Among its many honourable titles, the Koran describes itself as 'the criterion'. The sacred volume sets out a standard of right and wrong, distinguishes between guidance and error (Koran, chapter 2, v.256). The Muslim conscience, schooled in its idioms, adopts its iconoclastic temper as its own on every occasion. Muhammad, as the paradigmatic Muslim, is counselled to enjoin what is right and forbid what is evil throughout his prophetic career. Rushdie's attack on the authoritative integrity of a fallible Koran is therefore part of a much larger indictment of Islam as a faith which routinely and regularly confuses good with evil, divine with diabolic imperative. And yet with respect to a religion that uniquely continues to distinguish itself for its totally uncompromising emphasis on the distinction between right and wrong, such an indictment is at once ridiculously ironic and radically offensive.

6

There are a number of historical inaccuracies in *The Satanic Verses*. One of them is hugely significant. In the novel Rushdie makes his namesake, Salman—the first Persian convert to Islam—embrace the new faith in Mecca. Salman becomes the illiterate Prophet Mahound's trusted scribe; dissatisfied with the sacred writ, Salman decides to test the authenticity of the alleged revelations by interweaving his own work with that of Mahound's God. 'I was writing the Revelation and nobody was noticing' (p.368). First he changes minor details—and Mahound fails to notice; Salman subsequently makes major changes in law and doctrine—and Mahound still fails to notice the alterations. Disillusioned with the Prophet and the puritanical Muslim culture of Medina, Salman becomes an apostate, goes back to the hedonistic metropolis of Jahilia and launches a bitter ideological assault on the ungrateful Mahound and his absurdly evil teachings.

Rushdie takes considerable liberties with the biography of the historical character Salman al-Farsi. Salman actually converted to Islam in the early part of the Prophet's ministry in Medina and remained loyal to Muhammad all his life. Muhammad was unduly fond of Salman, often referring to him as his family, though Salman was not an Arab.

Thus, according to Rushdie, Salman the Persian, for whom Arabic was a foreign tongue, writes the Koran as he pleases and no one notices the changes. Muslim indignation is not altogether unjustified. (Ironically, Rushdie, through his namesake Salman, predicts his own fate at the hands of outraged Muslims, for Salman knows that blasphemy cannot go unpunished.) Muslim sensibilities have been sharply provoked by Rushdie's allegations about the textual impurity of the Koran. No piece of sacred literature has been so carefully preserved in its original language as the Arabic Koran. The early community felt, with reverence and awe, that these revelations vouchsafed to Muhammad were inimitably miraculous—the literal and infallible word of Allah, to be carefully preserved and transmitted to future generations. The canon of the Koran was already established at the time of Muhammad's death and, unlike the Bible, it has not undergone even the smallest change. Indeed even unintelligible letters, prefixed to certain chapters, are scrupulously reproduced as part of the revealed text up to this day.

Why does Rushdie create the character Salman by a total reversal of the biography of the historical character Salman al-Farsi? Some apocryphal sources suggest that Muhammad did employ an amanuensis who subsequently doubted the revelations and became an apostate. Could Rushdie be conflating two different historical characters? At any rate, it is hard to resist the suspicion that Rushdie invents a mouthpiece to launch a bitter diatribe against Islam and all things Islamic. In Gibreel's dreams, it is Salman who utters the most profane and vulgar remarks about Mahound and his religion. Muslims have often complained that Rushdie calls Abraham a bastard; to which defenders of Rushdie have retorted that it is Hagar, not Rushdie, who does so (p.95). But such a defence is considerably weaker in the case of Rushdie's namesake Salman. For Salman seems to have been created specifically to parody the principles of Islam.

Salman tells the anti-Islamic poet Baal about his experience with Muhammad that 'the closer you are to a conjurer, the easier to spot the trick'. And again on the same page, 'Mahound has no time for scruples . . . no qualms about ends and means' (p.363). Mahound 'laid down the law and the angels would confirm it afterwards' (p.365). Salman detests the comprehensive rules of the *Shari'ah* (Islamic law); laws for everything, 'all those revelations of convenience' (p.365). Rushdie, through Salman, invents a few new rules himself (pp.363–5): 'Sodomy and the missionary position were approved of by the archangel, whereas the forbidden postures included all those in which the female was on top' (p.364). The angel Gibreel lists forbidden and permitted topics of conversation, and specifies parts of the body which should never be scratched even if these itch uncomfortably, and so on.

7

Good writers exercise integrity not only in their choice of theme but also once they have chosen it. Rushdie fails on the latter score. The theme of revelation is central to Islam; and Rushdie has every right to give 'a secular, humanist vision of the birth of a great world religion'. Indeed a plausible secular account of revelation would be an indispensable part of any radical reservation about the Islamic outlook. But *The Satanic Verses* fails to offer a convincing account of the prophetic experience interpreted from a disbelieving perspective.

Rushdie does not necessarily intend to deny the power of revealed messages. His central aim is to explain—and perhaps explain away—the prophetic experience. In a pre-publication interview, Rushdie conceded that, as a disbeliever, he rejected the traditional model of the divine word descending on an illiterate prophet. Yet Rushdie claims that he does not wish to dismiss the recipient as a straightforward liar. How, then, is the allegedly sacred experience to be interpreted? Is it simply self-deception? Can one have a perceptive secular account of revelation that takes it seriously yet denies the recipient's own claim about its supernatural origins and causation? Predictably Rushdie opts for the view that the revelatory act is ultimately one extremely fertile form of the purely human imagination. To explore that form in a literary context is part of his professed task in *The Satanic Verses*.

If these are Rushdie's aims, there can be no question that he fails to achieve them. Mahound, the recipient of the sacred message, emerges as an insincere impostor who self-induces revelation whenever it suits him. He is a calculating opportunist devoid of conscience, making and breaking rules as he pleases, confusing (or perhaps deliberately identifying) good with evil as the mood takes him. Yet this clever and unscrupulous 'prophet' is easily fooled by his secretary who manages to contaminate the allegedly revealed message with a purely human contribution.

This is hardly a plausible or convincing account of the experience of a seminal prophetic figure. For it raises far more questions than it resolves. Can an insincere man be the founder of a major religious and moral tradition that outlives him? If Muhammad had been seen, by those who began to follow him, as cynical and unscrupulous, would Islam ever have achieved prominence on the stage of world history? Is an insincere Muhammad more convincing than a sincere one? Is an insincere and mistaken Muhammad more convincing than a sincere but mistaken one?

Rushdie's failure to achieve the more ambitious metaphysical goals is much more evident. *The Satanic Verses* falls short of convincing us that revelation cannot set out plausible moral norms for the human world. In Mahound's book, good and evil are indistinguishable. But we have only Rushdie's word for it. To show that good and evil are, as Nietzsche would say, merely prejudices, albeit God's prejudices, requires far more than merely a dramatic dogmatism.

8

The Satanic Verses is written in a language that is at times gratuitously obscene and wounding. In the controversial sections about Mahound, the locales Rushdie selects are almost always sexually suggestive in an immoral way and sometimes even degrade human nature. Much of the abuse, though, is straightforwardly explicit. Bilal, Khalid and Salman, who are three of Mahound's most distinguished companions, emerge as drunkards, idlers, and fools, 'the trinity of scum', 'that bunch of riff raff', 'fucking clowns'. (pp.101, 117, 374). Mahound himself is portrayed as a debauched sensualist, a drunkard given to self-indulgence (p.120). He is depicted lying naked and unconscious in Hind's tent with a hangover (pp.119–21). There are provocative scenes with Mahound and Hind (p.120), and with Mahound and the angel of revelation (p.122), with Baal and Mahound's wives in a brothel (pp.379–88).

Rushdie, like many modern authors, clearly rejects the traditional literary convention which authorises only the use of soft and domesticated language even in descriptions of a harsh, ugly, or otherwise disturbing reality. But even if we make allowances for that, the choice of idiom remains both unsuited to the theme and at times unnecessarily self-indulgent.

It is Rushdie's use of medieval Christian terminology that has most deeply outraged Muslim sensibilities. In the Middle Ages, Mahound was a devil believed to have composed the Arabic Koran. Muhammad was often referred to as Mahound because Christians took him to be a false prophet. Here is Rushdie's justification for his use of Mahound: 'To turn insults into strengths, whigs, tories, and blacks all chose to wear with pride the names they were given in scorn; likewise, our mountain-climbing prophet-motivated solitary is to be the medieval baby-frightener. The Devil's synonym: Mahound.' (p.93).

Let us examine Rushdie's contention. Now it is possible to accept, even with pride, that one is for example black, but it is harder to endorse a self-description such as 'black bastard' since the word 'bastard' is no mere description. It is a term of abuse. Similarly, at least on the face of it, it seems that one cannot, with understanding, wear the name Mahound with justified pride. For it is morally unintelligible for any self-respecting individual to see himself as the Devil.

The point is important. Take, for example, George Bernard Shaw's play *The Devil's Disciple*. Here the central character proudly calls himself 'the Devil's disciple'. But Shaw uses this as a shock tactic—to question the empty religiosity and self-righteousness of the 'Christian' protagonists. Theirs is a worship due to fear, not love. At least the Devil is brave enough to stand up to God—in order to assert his integrity as a dissenting critic of the Almighty and his mysterious ways. 'The Devil's disciple' emerges in the play as the truly religious man: he is charitable and willing to sacrifice his life in the hour of trial. The allegedly religious people come out very badly—craving for comfort and security. In *The Satanic Verses*, however, Mahound has no redeeming qualities. He is not merely mistakenly thought to be evil; he is actually evil through and through.

In his perceptive review of Rushdie's novel, Ali Mazrui quite rightly denies the usual parallel drawn between *The Satanic Verses* and *The Last Temptation of Christ* (*Ithaca Times*, 2–8 March 1989). The film 'accepts Christ as holy, respects the essential goodness of Jesus, then sees his godness (*sic*) competing with his humanity.' Mazrui goes on to say that this may amount to blasphemy for the Christian viewer but it is not necessarily abusive. *The Satanic Verses*, however, portrays Muhammad as fundamentally evil. No good impulses redeem his evil inclinations. (Think here of Machado de Assis's profound story 'The Devil's Church' in which Satan fails to find a perfect disciple since even the most corrupt human beings have some good in them.) The *Last Temptation of Christ* would be analogous to Rushdie's book if, for example, the Virgin Mary were portrayed as a prostitute and Jesus as an illegitimate child who grew up to exult in his own wickedness; or indeed if, as the Muslim writer T. B. Irving suggests in his review (*Impact International*, 23 June–13 July 1989), the disciples of Jesus were to be depicted as a gang of homosexuals given to gay orgies in the Garden of Gethsemane.

9

Though much of *The Satanic Verses* is incoherent and apparently unmotivated, the dream sequences, in which the tenets of Islam are ridiculed, retain complexity, motivation, and coherence. Here Rushdie freely adds to the existing stock of Western prejudices against the religion of the Arabian Prophet. Most of the unoriginal biases of traditional Christian polemic are resurrected in one form or another. Thus, for example, the myth of Muhammad's epilepsy—motivated historically by Christian fanaticism—is transferred unaccountably to Ayesha, the namesake of the Prophet's favourite wife. And there is slander too. Rushdie has Gibreel confirming that a man will never walk on the moon—which is reminiscent of the old Western fabrication about Muhammad preposterously requesting a mountain to come to him.

For Muslims Mecca was a city of ignorance before the light of the new faith; for Rushdie it remains more decidedly a city of ignorance after Islam (p.95). Under Mahound's rule the metropolis is steeped in sexual puritanism, Fascism, and hypocrisy. The converts to the new religion are insincere opportunists. Mahound outlaws all thought: whores, writers and poets will never be forgiven, according to his book.

There is a sustained attack on values such as chastity and modesty too. In a brothel, provocatively called *The Veil* (pp.379–88), the prostitutes assume the names and roles of Mahound's wives. The anti-Islamic poet Baal becomes the husband of the wives of the 'businessman prophet'. The prostitutes comically enact the domestic and political life of Mahound : 'the allegiances in the brothel came to mirror the political cliques at the Yathrib mosque' (p.382).

The brothel scene is of course purely imaginary; even Christian polemicists have drawn the line at this kind of insult. Unlike his Western supporters, Rushdie himself writes with an insider's awareness of the outrage such a portrayal would cause. Muhammad's spouses are instructed, by the Koran, to remain unmarried after their husband's death so that they can assume the honorific title, 'the mothers of the believers'. Muslims have reacted to what they interpret to be a straight-forwardly personal attack.

The Muslim anger at the brothel scenes is not properly explicable as being due to mere prudery. It is not as though we have over a million Mary Whitehouses among us. Islam is not an anti-sensual faith; and sexual appetite has always been regarded as wholesome and good within certain limits. But Muslims are rightly troubled by Rushdie's speculations because these reinforce a stereotypical and false picture of Muslim sexuality. The West has produced its own fantastic and romanticised portrait of the sexual dimension of Islamic civilisation, a portrait that in turn feeds the very fantasies that helped to create it. Rushdie is merely exploiting the Western image of Muslim sexuality as exotic and untamed.

One has every right to be sceptical about the authenticity of the Koranic revelations vouchsafed to Muhammad. And there are valid doubts about the fairness of certain Islamic social norms, particularly those governing the lives of women. But slander or libel are not adequate substitutes for critique or reverent reservation. And no individual, much less a universal community, can be expected to remain silent in the face of such provocation.

10

In one of its rare tender moments, *The Satanic Verses* gives us a profound insight into the dangers of a false religion. The chapters entitled 'Ayesha' and 'Parting of the Arabian Sea' deal with a superstitious Indian prophetess, 'the girl of the butterflies', who wields charismatic authority over her devotees. This epileptic orphan called Ayesha—the namesake of the Prophet's favourite spouse—believes that she is divinely authorised to lead her entire village on a miraculous pilgrimage on foot through the sea to Mecca. The sea fails to part; the believing crowd is drowned.

This is Rushdie's comment on superstitious religious conviction coming to grief in a modern world in which the rational techniques of empirical science claim greater reasonableness. The fictional account is based on the real Hawkes Bay tragedy of 1983 in Karachi, Pakistan. A Shi'ite woman believed that she had received a revelation commanding her to cross the Arabian sea on foot to perform a pilgrimage to Shi'ah holy precincts in Iraq. The woman and her disciples were drowned.

Rushdie ably uses the incident to condemn the impotence of religion in an age in which experimental science yields techniques independent of transcendent miracle and supernatural aid. It is also a powerfully relevant comment on the prostitution of religion, particularly in cult form, which can lead to social catastrophe.

Though Rushdie's exploration here is largely fair, one still needs to take exception to the possible implication that *all* religion is essentially superstition. For the distinction between true religion and false religion is available within a reflective religion. It is not in general necessary for believers to convert to socialism in order to see their own failings. There are resources internal to faith for sifting superstition from authentic conviction.

The Muslim may fairly object that Islam is not some cult or short-lived illusion. To be sure, some cynic might reply: it was a cult once upon a time, and it is a permanent illusion. Perhaps. But it is now an established religious tradition of proven and profound genius and vitality. It has been sifted by experience and history; it has antiquity of tradition, moral appeal, and countless adherents. Islam clearly satisfies deep human needs and produces a characteristic quality of allegiance. Only prejudice could deny that this religion has produced some men and women of character. None of this entails that Islam is true; and, to be sure, Islam has also produced superstition, narrow-hearted dogma and appalling obscurantism. Rushdie has every right—indeed a duty—to take Muslims to task on this score. He has the right to observe how such deplorable consequences are not merely due to the failings of Muslim humanity but are also perhaps implicit in Islamic dogma as enshrined in the Koran and the Muhammadan exemplar.

11

Theistic religion is a fundamental and fertile aspect of human life and thought, and has been so throughout recorded history. It is no coincidence that so many significant — including Nobel prize winning — works of fiction have dealt with themes such as God, the Devil, good and evil. Among Muslim writers, Najib Mahfuz's *The Children of the Man of the Mountain* is a landmark in the history of reverent scepticism about Islamic conviction. Muhammad Kamil Hussain's enigmatic *The City of Evil* is a highly original account of the events of Good Friday.

Within the Islamic world, there are established traditions of controversialism and critique of traditional conviction, notwithstanding the pressures from a rigid orthodoxy that often outlaws enquiry and debate. But none of these traditions moves beyond legitimate satire and sustained criticism into forms of parody and caricature wholly motivated by indignation and hatred. There is a proper recognition, unavoidably forced upon people in the Middle Eastern context, that religious, like sexual, themes are dangerously elemental. We need to handle them with care and due understanding, though even a scepticism reverent in tone may be iconoclastic in its content.

To avoid the censorship of law or, more informally, the censorship of burning and, more extremely, the censorship of assassination, one needs to exercise caution. But the caution is not due to fear. It is due to courtesy. If one enters other people's sanctuary, it is as well to take off one's shoes.

Rushdie enters the mosque — but tactlessly refuses to take off his shoes. (In one of the scenes in *The Satanic Verses*, the characters are incongruously playing rock and roll music in the mosque!) But even as a strategy, it is wise to show courtesy. If we are to get people to understand the factors that figure in their making, their anxieties, their hopes, it cannot be right for us to ignore these factors ourselves. Rushdie should enter the Islamic sanctuary with respect for his opponents as people, albeit people with false notions in their heads. Once in it, let him argue as he will. Let him even show

30

anger on behalf of a sincere if frustrated humanitarianism.
The quality and motivation of our quarrel with others matters.
Is it out of love or malice? Rushdie may well be motivated
by sympathy for these misguided fellow human beings. But
we can hardly guide others if we lose the way ourselves.

Rushdie cannot flatter himself with the conceit that he has
properly indulged the sceptical temper, although one would
indeed think, judging from the comments of his Western
admirers, that he was ploughing a virgin field. Yet sceptics
there have been and always will be. What matters is the
quality and integrity of their doubts. A Job-like attempt,
reverent and sincere, to cut the gods down to our size, is
found in many Islamic thinkers and novelists, all the way
from the great al-Ghazzali to our Muhammad Iqbal and Najib
Mahfuz. Within Rushdie's unprincipled prose, one looks in
vain for the penetrating critique of a Mahfuz implying tragi-
cally that occasional divine tuition via messengership (in the
Islamic style) does not suffice, human perversity being invet-
erate as it is.

At the end of the day, *The Satanic Verses* fails to raise the
truly central issues about a distinctively Muslim identity in
the contemporary world of varied voices and irreligious con-
fidences. It fails to set the agenda for the Islamic Enlightenment—a Muslim response to modernity. That agenda can
only properly be set by Muslim intellectuals who are believers
and who are themselves disturbed by the widespread and
apparently reasonable secular reservations about the religious
imagination in the age of reason.

12

'When we are born', says Rushdie movingly in an interview
in December 1988, 'we are not automatically human beings.
We have to learn how to be human. Some of us get there
and some of us don't.' In *The Satanic Verses*, none of the
Muslim characters gets there. Gibreel Farishta, the symbol
of the good, loses his faith and eventually commits suicide.
Chamcha, the unlikely hero of the novel, eventually makes
it. Though he is the symbol of evil in much of the novel,

31

Chamcha acquires goodness because of a single act of brav-
ery. He discovers himself truly when he re-adopts his Indian
identity by a pure act of the will. Chamcha gets there because,
in Rushdie's words, 'he faces up to the big things like love
and death'. Chamcha's father also emerges as a hero. He is
portrayed as a courageous life-long secularist who does not
contaminate his atheism even by a death-bed conversion to
Islam.

A strong undercurrent in *The Satanic Verses* is the idealised
and totally unconvincing portrayal of atheists and secularists.
This is in conscious contrast to crassly offensive images of
fundamentalists, particularly Muslim fundamentalists: the
martyr Imam as a pure form of evil, devouring people like a
snake; the fundamentalist preacher in a Bombay mosque who
encourages a mob to stone to death an innocent but illegitimate infant; and the preacher in a Delhi mosque who incites
sectarian violence and is unusually fond of wealth. (Rushdie
even drops the pretence in chapter 8 that some of these
portraits are in Gibreel's dream sequences.)

All great writers achieve triumphs of portraiture whether
comic, religious, or female—as in Dickens, Greene and
Hardy respectively. There are no triumphs of religious
portraiture in any of Rushdie's novels. Chamcha is as unconvincing as Gibreel. Chamcha rejects Islam but this is not a
reflective or turbulent act; Islam was never a part of his or
his family's outlook. And Gibreel Farishta simply loses his
faith when his prayers for a cure for his mysterious disease
fail to be answered. And this as if religious conviction were
straightforwardly an experimental matter. After a Western
education, Dr Aziz in *Midnight's Children* predictably
espouses atheism. There is an empty room where God once
lived. But Rushdie fails to convince us that Dr Aziz's loss of
traditional faith is conscientious, passionate, existentialist—
rather than merely fashionable and frivolous.

The question itself is among the most serious. Is there a
place in our hearts for the supernatural? Is there a godly
imprint on human nature? Explorations of these questions,
whether in factual or imaginative contexts, by Westernised
Indian, Pakistani and Egyptian writers tend to be shallow

and predictable. There is rarely an attempt to locate their seriousness within the Islamic tradition itself. Instead one finds an uncritical acceptance of the results of Western speculation on these issues. A writer will typically flirt with Eurocentric traditions of radical atheism and endorse their philosophical claims wholesale. I myself have never come across a single human being, whether fictional or real, from an educated élite Third World background, who was a *conscientious* atheist.

This is of course entirely to be expected. For one must experience the radical reservation for oneself, not merely borrow it, so to speak, from others. Atheists in the West have forged a tradition of rejection; many Jews and Christians, often from pious backgrounds, have experienced conscientious doubts about the truth of traditional theism. This is not true of atheists from a Muslim background. There has been no attempt to know and experience two radically opposed styles of living. For there is usually a strict commitment to only one tradition—namely, that of European atheistic humanism. One actually needs to feel the tension between a genuine commitment to Islamic conviction and the opposed demands of a lifestyle that seeks exemption from allegedly supernatural demands. The atheism of most writers and intellectuals from Third World backgrounds is due to an insincere and fashionable radicalism—and not, as they themselves imagine, a costly and discerning intellectual passion.

On 12 March 1989, the *Observer* published an anonymous letter, allegedly written by a Pakistani from Karachi who wanted to commit apostasy and who hailed Rushdie as his hero. He complained that atheists were persecuted in Muslim lands. Such a person is likely to belong to the wealthier secularised classes who regularly commit apostasy with impunity. The letter is almost certainly an attempt to gain sympathy from the Western reader by playing on his or her ignorance of Pakistani society. At any rate, we would need some strong evidence to suggest that his atheism was conscientiously espoused.

13

There is a prevalent myth among Western reviewers that somehow Rushdie is a deeply compassionate author, showing misguided Muslims the truth about themselves. But if one is to show people the mirror, to get them to understand the elements of their own make-up, one does not do well to begin by ignoring them oneself. To get people to see themselves for what they really are—as power-conscious, status-conscious, weak-willed, hypocritical, and eventually, merely human, all too human—one needs to take them gently by the hand. In these matters of self-scrutiny, one has every right to take the horse to water; but one cannot make it drink. Rushdie is wrong in thinking that shock tactics will do the trick. In the face of that, even the alert and thoughtful may withdraw into a more secure fortress of dogmatism and inherited security of mind and will.

It is in this context that we need to examine briefly the view that Rushdie is a distinguished anti-racist whose book is a compassionate and passionate account of the problems of contemporary Asians in Britain. Such a compassion would, it is argued, redeem Rushdie's allegedly harsh treatment of Islam. Despite the prodigiously massive prestige that is attached to his name in anti-racist circles, I find it hard to believe that Rushdie has any real understanding of the daily headaches many ordinary blacks experience in this country.

For one thing, it cannot be any part of his experience. He came to an English public school, then Cambridge—hardly the experience of the people on whose behalf he campaigns. To be sure, one shouldn't exaggerate the importance of this limitation. For his sympathy could none the less be genuine and discerning. But does he understand the worries over, say, DNA testing, laws that separate families, the poverty of immigrants newly arrived to an alien and hostile culture, the inarticulate blacks' helplessness with language? His own experience of racism is the experience of privileged Asians up against subtle forms of that evil—say at public school or an Oxbridge college. But that is certainly not the experience of racism for most ordinary Asians settled in the inner city areas of Bradford or Birmingham.

14

That *The Satanic Verses* is blasphemous should be, for the Muslim conscience, uncontroversial. There has been much talk, by confused Muslims and their non-Muslim mentors, of the complexity of the Islamic tradition, of the variety of proper responses to Rushdie's work. Given that the Koran is the book which defines the authentically Muslim outlook, there is no choice in the matter. And it is for Muslims to interpret the imperatives of their own religion. Any Muslim who fails to be offended by Rushdie's book ceases, on account of that fact, to be a Muslim. *The Satanic Verses* has become a litmus-paper test for distinguishing faith from rejection. The test applies to all shades of opinion—orthodox, heretical, indifferent; it applies to all Muslims—good, bad, practising, lapsed. The sacrilege of *The Satanic Verses* ought to be experienced as offensive even by believers for whom Islam is merely their idleness—or conscience—on Friday afternoons. These contentions are completely conclusive; there is no room here for private sophistication rooted in hypocrisy and schooled in dishonesty. And God is well aware of the things we do.

Rushdie leaves too many clues in *The Satanic Verses* to show that unprincipled abuse rather than disciplined critique was his dominant intention. (This is why, incidentally, one cannot take his novel seriously as a powerful work of art.) For Muslims, the Rushdie affair is not a matter of Western freedom in conflict with Islamic control but rather Western licence to ridicule in conflict with an Islamic emphasis on disciplined and reverent criticism. The attempt to debase and degrade sacred or deeply held convictions should be resolutely challenged.

Most Muslims have been critical of their own tradition and willing to enter into debate. This is a point that bears repetition. Muslim historians have been thorough recorders of their own tradition, honestly setting down all known facts and thus leaving a rich source of material for later critics, whether

Muslim or non-Muslim. Even in the scholarly tradition, many writers have interpreted the same material in radically opposed ways. No one has burnt orientalist treatises against Islam, though many are inferior in their argument and typically full of sentiments that border on hatred.

In bringing this chapter to a close, let us return to the theme with which it opened. 'You write a book', says Rushdie, 'and governments fall—that never happens.' Perhaps not. But one can write a book—and people get killed. It would be absurd to suggest that *The Satanic Verses* directly caused the deaths of Muslim demonstrators. But controversial writing can incite anger, and such anger is a contributing factor in violent conflict. Polemical traditions have had accompanying wars in which the joint restraints of scholarship and civilisation have been thrown off. Christian-Muslim rivalry is not restricted to academic journals; the streets of Beirut refute any such assumption.

Controversial books can cause wars—not necessarily because they preach in its favour but because even divinely inspired doctrines, in frail human custody, are liable to be misunderstood. How much more so in the case of our human, all too human, writings. The pen, in the wrong hands, is no less dangerous than the sword.

3 The Liberal Inquisition

1

'Most of our problems begin', said Salman Rushdie in a pre-publication interview, 'when people try to define the world in terms of a stark opposition between good and evil.' This is a perceptive comment that may well apply to the controversy over his own book. From an early stage the entire Western press stereotyped the peaceful Muslim protests as anti-intellectual, indeed Fascist, attempts to curtail democratic freedoms of speech and thought dear to the Western conscience. To be sure, there were many empty warnings that, in W. L. Webb's words (*Guardian*, 17 February 1989), the Rushdie affair must not be reduced 'to a simple neo-Victorian opposition between our light and their darkness'. But, in practice, virtually every Western commentator paid lip-service to this demand and succumbed to temptation. For it is impossible, particularly in retrospect, to remain unimpressed by the high and holy tones of those who wrote in defence of Rushdie's rights, threatened by the encroachments of an allegedly barbaric and intolerant creed.

For several months, both Muslims and their opponents were transported into a bygone age of passion and heresy. Freedom crusades began in earnest and set out for the House of Islam. Accusations and rejoinders abounded; the obscurantism of the Muslims had to be countered with Western enlightenment. It was indeed our light and their darkness. There could hardly have been a better setting for The Liberal Inquisition.

2

Immediately after the publication of Rushdie's novel in late September 1988 in London, Western Muslims began to write to Viking seeking an appointment. Petitions were sent to the London and New York offices requesting a dialogue with the publishers. I myself sent a lengthy 'Open Letter Concerning Blasphemy', subsequently published in a British theological journal. The enquirers, whether Islamic organisations or individual Muslims, all received the same response. In their letter, the publishers replied that the outrage and accusations of blasphemy were both due to a misunderstanding. The passages involving Islam and the Prophet were all in dream sequences, dreamt by a character often described as insane and indeed destined for suicide. These dreams do not purport to reflect real events in Muhammad's biography. *The Satanic Verses*, was, then, the Muslims were reassured, a fictional work of great profundity, wrapped in applause by Western literary critics. There was no question of negotiations, let alone of a withdrawal or ban.

The response of Muslims the world over was reasoned and unduly restrained. Countless individual believers and Islamic organisations wrote letters and petitions to Viking throughout October and November 1988. Viking responded that they would not only continue to publish *The Satanic Verses* but also had plans to translate it into nine other major languages. Several Muslim groups, prominently the Islamic Defence Council in London and the National Da'wah Committee of the USA in Chicago, pressed for an interview with the publishers to explain the Muslim objections. But Viking turned a deaf ear to all such requests.

Muslims, unaware of finer points of the laws of the United Kingdom, began to threaten legal action against the publishers—or, if the publishers were indemnified, then against Rushdie. There was talk of a financial boycott of all Penguin publications. In all major British cities with Muslim populations, outraged Muslims met, argued, discussed and went back home frustrated. They met again and again. At the Bradford Council of Mosques, we burnt the midnight oil— every night. A concerned leadership emphasised moderation and patience. Given that there was no single authority to supervise so populous and heterogeneous a community as the Muslims even in Britain, many influential Muslims feared an outburst of sacred rage against Rushdie and Penguin personnel.

While Muslim groups and organisations met regularly to form committees that would formulate long-term strategies, Muslim writers, on both sides of the Atlantic, began to offer detailed critiques of *The Satanic Verses*. Few ever appeared in print. The Western press had already firmly convinced themselves that even peaceful written Muslim protests were, ironically, a threat to freedom of speech and conviction. Accordingly, the media effectively endorsed an operative veto on any exploration of the grounds for 'fundamentalist' options in Islam.

In the early days of the affair a few Muslims managed to have letters published in the national papers and to appear on radio and television. To the charge that Muslims were opposed to freedom of speech, Muslims replied that such a freedom, like any other democratic liberty, ought to be exercised with due responsibility. The issue, properly speaking, the Muslims insisted, was not of freedom of speech versus censorship but rather of legitimate scepticism versus obscenity and slander. More or less all the Western critics merely parroted in response that freedom of speech was a very valuable and hard-won liberty for which the Western conscience had historically paid a high price. No one, Muslim or otherwise, they continued, would ever be allowed to usurp this right.

Rushdie himself was meanwhile being lionised by the literary establishment as well as by the ordinary freedom-loving peoples of the Western world. In many television and radio programmes as well as in articles in the national dailies, he described himself (and was uncritically taken to be) a courageous and liberal *Muslim* daring to confront the obscurantism and rigid authoritarianism of a fundamentalist minority currently agitating the Islamic masses throughout the globe.

All criticism of his stance was silenced by the truly remarkable rejoinder that no Muslim had read the book. Presumably there must be some Muslims in the world who can read and who can appreciate literature. Suppose one had read the book, remarkable a feat as that is (though, to be sure, not for the reasons Rushdie or his admirers might suggest). More-

over it is not a necessary condition of having knowledge of a
work that one should have read it, any more than it is necessary for a judge to witness a murder in order to pass judgement. The ordinary Muslim went by the verdict of those
trusted religious and other learned authorities who had read
the whole book, much as a judge goes by the evidence sup-
plied by eye-witness accounts. That the liberal opponents of
the Muslim stance should resort to such weak and indeed
fallacious reasoning has always struck me as crucially revealing. Western animus against Islam and all things Islamic runs
deep indeed in the groove of cultural and historical memory.

No other artistic or intellectual issue of recent decades has
received so extensive a coverage from the mainstream British,
indeed Western, media as the Rushdie affair. At one time,
the matter received so much official attention that it became
a point of daily conversation at all levels of society. Every
serious British (and French and American) publication has
dealt with the Rushdie affair on its front pages and in its
editorials as well as making it the subject of many special
features and articles. Yet for all that, Western commentary
can safely be seen, even by non-Muslims in retrospect, as
shallow and extravagant. To be sure, some newspaper and
television coverage was investigative and balanced. But over-
whelmingly it was accusatory in its very format, inviting hasty
and unoriginal judgement against the Muslims. In Britain, as
in France and the United States, the gutter press incited
Westerners against Islam, using familiar racist and Fascist
methods of stereotypical depiction, presenting Rushdie's
book as an accurate portrayal of the Islamic faith. Oddly
enough, the quality papers differed from such papers as the
Sun and the *News of the World* mainly in their choice of more
sophisticated language, since the content was substantially
identical.

It was indeed a winter of discontent for the Muslims of
Britain. Countless writers, who might otherwise be credited
with a measure of compassion, began openly to mock and
insult the beliefs and traditions of Islam—that exotic creed
close yet far from the Christian West. The Koran was frequently being quoted out of context; liberal-sounding tra-

ditions of the Prophet Muhammad, recommending charity and scholarship, were being cited to justify Rushdie's book. All Islamic doctrines suddenly became fair game; writers and editors who confessed to know nothing about Islam freely threw away the restraints of objectivity and diplomacy: this intolerant and oppressive creed mutilated the rights of women, its penal code incorporated Draconian rulings that shocked the civilised (an alternative for Western) conscience. Liberal resentment began to flood the publications. Everywhere, everyone had the right to attack Islam and the Muslims. After all, didn't the Muslim reaction to Rushdie's book justify this righteous indignation?

For the media, Islam, particularly fundamentalist Islam, as they defined it, has long been a legitimate object of both fascination and uncritical accusation. The Rushdie saga had an ideal recipe for excitement: a distinguished author driven into hiding by a wicked Muslim fanatic, oil sheikhs, veiled women, and newspaper secretaries hesitating over the *kh* in Khomeini and other chaps with equally unspellable names. Unfortunately, however, fascination is not an adequate substitute for knowledge.

Every evening, one came home to watch the news—and catch the name of a new expert on Islam. Christian experts, Jewish experts, Hindu experts, Marxist experts, agnostic experts, to name a few. Every kind of expert—except a Muslim expert. Presumably Muslim fanatics cannot be expected to attain the measure of detachment Westerners consider necessary for objectivity. It rarely occurred to anyone that those who reject Islam may also fail in their obligation to be fair—for different reasons. After Khomeini's intervention, one saw a new round of experts on 'Iranian Islam'—whatever that expression is supposed to mean. All the experts were, unsurprisingly, Iranian exiles as well known for their atheism as for their hostility to Khomeini.

Finally they came, the so-called Muslim experts. The creators of Western opinion about the religion of Islam have always displayed much ingenuity in finding allegedly Muslim spokesmen whom authentic Muslims rightly reject as failing to be even believers, let alone representatives of authoritative opinion. Both in the media and the university departments, the spokesmanship of the Muslim cause is almost invariably confined to liberal or Judaeo-Christian expertise. Where Muslim representatives do appear they are, without exception, either simplistic believers ignorant of (and therefore incapable of challenging) Western traditions of thought or else Third World champagne socialists passionately repudiating the faith of their forebears. Now that we had heard everyone, would anyone listen to the Muslims themselves?

3

Many of the consequences of the Muslim reaction to the publication of *The Satanic Verses* have been unintended ones which could not have reasonably been foreseen. For example, the Rushdie affair has eventually generated a context in which the age-old Western veto on any authentic representation of Islam has been effectively broken—for the first time. It did not happen overnight. But the days of the so-called experts on Islam are indeed numbered; the spokesmanship for the Islamic cause has finally fallen, at least partly and temporarily, into the hands and mouths of authentic and able Muslim believers.

The Liberal Inquisition was set to continue throughout the West for several months before serious debate could begin. In the early days, notwithstanding loud professions of freedom of speech, there were many editors who systematically prohibited *all* Muslim contributions to their publications. Anger and frustration among Muslims grew; a minority denied access to power and control finally resorted to public protest—itself a conclusive proof of powerlessness.

In December 1988 about 500 Muslims in Bradford gathered to listen to the offending passages from *The Satanic Verses*. I had sought a dispensation from the religionists that would enable me to read the blasphemous sections without sin or guilt, purely for purposes of educating the Muslim believers. Though I took great care to censor some of the more profane suggestions, I was physically prevented from reading even some of the censored materials by a number of outraged

Muslims in the audience—one of whom fainted with anger. It became rapidly clear to the Bradford Council of Mosques that only a dramatic ritual would ease the frustration and vent the profound anger of the believing community. Accordingly it was resolved that a copy of *The Satanic Verses* be burnt publicly in front of the Bradford City Hall.

When Rushdie's book was burnt in mid-January 1989 hardly anyone thought the event was worth reporting. The incident, however, was destined to become famous. Once Khomeini had issued his edict calling for the execution of the author and the publishers, a whole tribe of journalists suddenly arrived in Bradford. It was only then that Westerners were actively concerned to know why the Muslims had burnt the book. In fact, an earlier burning in Bolton (on 2 December 1988) was doomed to remain obscure and largely unreported. Bradford had become, partly as an accident of timing, the newly discovered citadel of Muslim radicalism.

The Bradford book-burning incident in mid-January acquired retrospective significance as Khomeini intervened one month later. How short the journey, mused Western moralists, between burning the book and burning the author! It was a sad reminder of former days. In England, as recently as the end of the nineteenth century, literature judged to be seditious or blasphemous was burned, in lieu of the author, by the public hangman. In a *Daily Telegraph* editorial (17 January 1989) the Bradford book-burning was dubbed a reaction 'in the fashion of the ayatollahs'. White liberal resentment flooded the papers; the Nazi-style book-burning was judged an act so dark and medieval that British Muslims were invited to behave according to civilised contemporary Western standards. An old-age pensioner from Wales wrote to the Bradford Council of Mosques a long letter (addressed, incidentally, to 'The Muslim Fanatics') in which she reassured us that her husband had not fought in two world wars in vain.

The Muslims rightly retorted that the burning of offensive literature was not invented by Muslims. At the height of the Rushdie affair, Poll Tax registration forms were burnt by some left-wing groups, not to mention an earlier burning of an immigration document by MPs. Even an effigy of the

Environment Secretary, Nicholas Ridley, was set alight at a time when white and liberal resentment singled out Muslims for using uncivilised tactics in their campaign. Given that the style of British Muslim protest was not uniquely barbaric, it was fair to speculate that the resentment really centred around the fact that these foreigners—blacks, Muhammadans, immigrants—were taking liberties in someone else's country.

Instead of asking, compassionately, why reasonable men and women can be so outraged by the written word, leading articles even by otherwise thoughtful writers simply condemned the Muslims as Fascists and literary hooligans. Instead of asking why Muslims resorted to such desperate measures, the Liberal Inquisition turned its full fury on a powerless minority. After the Rushdie episode, Muslims are likely to harbour permanent doubts about the fairness and compassion of the liberal conscience.

Those were tense days, but not without humour if one looked carefully at the writing on the wall. Most of it is too cynical and unprintable. But some of it was revealing. One regularly saw variations of cartoons depicting worried mosque-going Islamic fundamentalists incongruously in book stores ordering, 'Two copies of *The Satanic Verses* and a box of matches'. A bad joke, of course, but how revealing in its implied commentary on the Muslims.

It was a sad irony indeed. The prevalent image of Islam as an anti-intellectualist faith is one of the several paradoxes generated by the Rushdie episode. For Islam is, in fact, a literary faith *par excellence*. Unlike Christianity and Judaism, it claims only one distinctive miracle—the Koran. For Muslims, the sacred scripture in Arabic is interpreted to be a miracle of reason and speech which supersedes the earlier 'sensual' miracles associated with the ministries of Muhammad's prophetic predecessors. References to the pen abound within the Koran; and Muslim civilisation has accordingly sanctioned a deep respect for scholarship. The ink of the scholar, as the Prophet famously said, is holier than the blood of the martyr.

After Khomeini issued his famous religious decree (*fatwa*)

in mid-February, Western resentment against Islam and the Muslims reached a peak. By late February, liberals and racists had found a common target. The Commission for Racial Equality issued its first public statement wholeheartedly condemning Khomeini and the Muslim outrage without any corresponding condemnation of the author or the publishers. The word 'Muslim' had become a term of abuse; there was an increase in racial tension in schools and public places. In Bradford, Sheffield, and London, mosques were stoned; there were minor incidents of racial violence.

Racist indignation flooded the daily papers; there were even calls for bans on immigration from Muslim countries. There was talk of deporting Muslims who publicly supported Khomeini's *fatwa*. Muslims were regularly portrayed as trouble-makers refusing to 'assimilate' while other ethnic groups were appropriately applauded for their good sense and cooperation. Many leading writers openly began to doubt the very possibility, let alone the wisdom, of creating a multicultural society in the first place. Britain had been too good, too kind, too tolerant of its Muslim minority. And the Muslims were ungrateful in interpreting toleration as a weakness; they remained scornful of the majority's tolerance, unwilling to reciprocate the respect and forbearance of the host culture. That those who preferred Iran to Britain should promptly leave was not an inference any Muslim ever needed to draw for himself.

The Liberal Inquisition was not restricted to the United Kingdom. The whole of the Western world was united in its rejection of Muslim demands for a state ban. The book was published simultaneously in Britain and Canada in September 1988. Sales were temporarily suspended in Canada to investigate whether or not it contravened the country's hate laws. As these laws were interpreted to be inapplicable to Muslims, it was decided that the book was acceptable, and sales continued despite large Muslim demonstrations in Toronto and Montreal in early March and smaller ones in other Canadian cities. Use of the Nathan Philip Square, the usual place for rallies, was denied by the Toronto City Council: a $2 million insurance condition was imposed and no insurance company was willing to offer such coverage. Many Canadian editorial writers openly condemned Islam and the Muslims; others in the media even proposed a ban on Muslims airing their views since Muslims wanted to deny Rushdie that right. The Canadian media gave the impression that Rushdie was a Canadian citizen whom Muslim barbarians were hunting in the peaceful streets of downtown Toronto or Montreal. Though the Canadian population is comprised entirely of immigrant groups settling at different dates, Canadian racists were still telling the Muslims to go to Iran if they disliked living in Canada.

In Canada's big neighbour to the south, the book was published in late February amid general condemnation of Khomeini's *fatwa* and the Bradford book-burning. It had already been reviewed in the *New York Times Book Review* in late January and in the *Washington Times* in mid-February. The reviews were not favourable. The *New York Times* reviewer wrote: 'How are we to understand the adoption— by a writer born Muslim—of so defamatory a name for the Prophet of Islam?' The *Washington Times* reviewer was even less sympathetic:

> But having discovered no literary reason why Mr Rushdie chose to portray Muhammad's wives as prostitutes, the Koran as the work of Satan and the founders of the faith as roughnecks and cheats, I had to admit to a certain sympathy with the Islamic leaders' complaints. True or not, slander hurts the slandered, which makes 'The Satanic Verses' not simply a rambling and trivial book, but a nasty one as well.

In the American reaction, it was clear from the outset that freedom of expression overrides the nature of the contents of the book—variously admitted to be trivial, incoherent, and even blasphemous. There followed a belligerent and concerted campaign in favour of freedom of speech. Muslims protested in large numbers throughout February and March in New York, Washington, San Francisco, and other cities; there were seminars and public lectures by Muslims in many university campuses, notably Berkeley and Cornell. But to no avail. It seemed that, for Americans, the freedom to blaspheme Islam is as holy and sacred as any Islamic sanctity. In

Atlanta, Georgia, a reading of *The Satanic Verses* was held at the Public Library on 25 February amid great publicity. Seven Muslim women in *hijab* (veil), and their three young children, entered the reading session and denounced Rushdie as a 'cultural pimp'.

The French reaction is significant. With a large North African Muslim population, Islam is the second largest faith in the country. The French press has been characterised by its passionately expressed and unconditional support for both *The Satanic Verses* and its author. Khomeini—who once successfully sought political asylum in France—has been copiously condemned at all levels of French society. Freedom of speech and conviction has been cited by virtually every French writer as an overriding principle of a free and democratic culture. The first French newspaper to print excerpts from the book was the influential *Figaro*, which added an unusual disclaimer to appease Muslim anger. Translated, it reads:

Figaro in publishing excerpts from Rushdie's book does not adopt its ideas as its own. We publish these with the exclusive aim of keeping our readers informed. While Islam should be respected as are other religions such as Christianity and Judaism, so too should the right of an author to express his freedom of expression be respected.

Figaro published selections from *The Satanic Verses* in late February. Within days, the weekly magazine *Nouvel Observateur* followed suit as did the daily newspaper *Libération*. These moves to publish offending quotations may well have been concerted—aiming to avoid Muslim reprisal against any single publication. *Nouvel Observateur* published a few interviews with angry Muslims who opposed Rushdie's book, seeing it as a serious attack on Islam and its sacred personalities. But the overwhelming majority of contributions betrayed a deep animus towards Islam and the Muslim stance on *The Satanic Verses*.

The popular French papers such as *France Soir* and *Paris Match* were also unequivocal in their condemnation of Muslim, especially Iranian, attitudes as barbaric and wicked. National indignation in France can perhaps only be appreciated if one adds in the balance the fact that French colonial memories of Algerian and North African Islam have been dramatically revived by the Rushdie affair.

Le Monde devoted many articles to the Rushdie saga over a number of days. Its editor-in-chief, André Fontaine, rejected Muslim indignation as misguided, and declared Rushdie to be a great and pioneering author, and *The Satanic Verses* a modern classic. This was, by and large, an unusual judgement. The bulk of the extensive French coverage has been focussed on the French and Western outcry against Muslim reaction and Khomeini's *fatwa*, rather than on the contents of the book or on the ability of its author. Many writers could certainly condemn Khomeini's verdict and other Muslim excesses without necessarily going to the extreme of endorsing Fontaine's flattering judgement about the novel and its author.

In the months that followed Khomeini's intervention, throughout the Western world *The Satanic Verses* was neither condemned nor banned. There was scant sympathy for the voiceless Muslim population resident in the West. In fact, the book was vehemently defended in the name of freedom of speech by everyone—liberals, Marxists, Christians, and Fascists alike. Throughout February and the months that followed there were plans to publish it in many European languages. France and Germany, along with some of the Scandinavian nations, went ahead despite initial fear and trembling. Spain had a multi-imprint edition with several leading publishers lending a helping hand. Brazil and Israel followed suit in the summer of 1989. The Liberal Inquisition was set to continue.

4

On 22 February 1989, Michael Ignatieff chaired a debate on the Rushdie affair for the BBC2 programme *The Late Show*. The eight protagonists included Muslim and non-Muslim writers and campaigners. I was among them. There was a broad range of opinion: all the Westerners—Edward Said, George Steiner, Ian MacEwan, and Michael Ignatieff himself— vigorously defended Rushdie's right to publish *The Satanic Verses*.

Shusha Guppy, the Iranian exile, Fadia Faqir, the Jordanian feminist writer, and Aziz al-Azmeh, the Syrian Christian teaching Islamic studies at Exeter University, all concurred with the non-Muslim participants and added that a Muslim need not be offended by the book. Dr Hesham el-Assawy of the Society for the Promotion of Religious Toleration condemned *The Satanic Verses* as a gratuitous provocation to Muslim sensibilities but did not condone its burning or removal from circulation. As the only fundamentalist Muslim in the debate, I was alone in condemning the book as an inferior piece of hate literature which the Bradford Muslims had rightly burned and hoped to see banned by state legislation. I ended my contribution with a plea to the media to lift its operative veto on any intellectual exploration of the grounds for fundamentalist options in religion.

I was lucky. My articles on the Rushdie affair appeared in the *Guardian* in late February and in the *Observer* on Easter Sunday. In what have since been widely interpreted to be apologias for Islamic fundamentalism, I argued for the position that *The Satanic Verses* should be banned because it reinforces prejudice against an already maltreated religious minority. Islam, as a unified enterprise of faith and power, was a charter for Muslim political life; it could not properly be reduced to merely an item of personal piety in the private sector. The term 'fundamentalism' was, I argued, invariably used in a propagandist sense to discredit the Muslims' legitimate political ambitions and impose upon them an alien kind of piety, borrowed from the post-Enlightenment Christian model. Muslims had every right to defend their faithful heritage in an aggressively secular society that daily encroached on religious sanctities. In such a context, any faith which compromised its internal temper of constructive if militant wrath was destined for the dustbin of history.

The reactions to my pieces on fundamentalism were very revealing. While some of the letters I received were thoughtful and probing, the majority of those who wrote suggested that I leave the country. Several individuals referred to me as a Fascist, the British Ayatollah seeking to establish a theocracy in the middle of Yorkshire with Iranian support. To

'The Ayatollah's Bradford acolyte, Dr Shabbir Akhtar' was the only form of address on the envelope of one unsigned letter of undisclosed origin which, thanks to the efficiency of the postal system, arrived successfully at my house one morning. It was a typical attack in which my claims were made to stand on their head. The next time there are gas chambers in Europe, it will in fact be Dr Akhtar and the Ayatollahs who will be operating them—and the liberals and Rushdie's supporters would be inside them! The writer of the letter, like a quarter of all the correspondents, concealed his or her identity and address because 'unlike Rushdie, I won't take chances with my life'.

There were published responses too. Michael Foot's attack (*Guardian*, 10 March 1989) in which he absurdly elevated Rushdie to an historical figure, was influential and, paradoxically, written with the very temper of 'militant wrath' which he condemned in my essay. In my response, I argued that Foot was using 'fundamentalist' in a pejorative sense and that, in any case, he was not sufficiently knowledgeable to judge the merits of the Muslim case against Rushdie. As for the Third World champagne socialists whom Foot so passionately admired, these are, I maintained, 'a people of low intelligence, devoid of conscience'. It is a harsh judgement—but it is wholly true. A conscientious and sincere atheism is worthy of respect; a fashionable repudiation of Islam undertaken primarily to impress a liberal Anglo-European audience is not. One critic, thoroughly incensed by the admittedly arrogant tone of my response, wondered whether I had been 'awarded a doctorate for a thesis on verbal abuse'. I was not as richly rewarded as Salman Rushdie: Fay Weldon has recently canonised him for a similar talent.

The range and quality of accusation varied. But both in private correspondence and published response, several critics condemned the logic of fundamentalist conviction and ambition as 'grotesque', and my claims as essentially empty rhetoric designed to agitate Muslims and offend non-Muslims. There were blanket condemnations of militant fundamentalist Islam as an intolerant creed designed to oppress women in Muslim societies, deny basic human rights in countries like

Iran, suppress scholarship and creativity, and, here at home, create tensions in an already strained multi-cultural British society. I was branded simply as an apologist for an indefensible outlook.

Behind the scenes, private uncertainty began to grow. Did the fundamentalist Muslims have a case after all? Were the Bradford Muslims really a bunch of ignorant peasants as the 'moderate' Muslims would have us believe? Wasn't it high time that Muslims themselves were allowed to be spokesmen for their own cause? One began to hear authentic Muslim voices on the radio and see Muslim faces on the television with some regularity. The so-called moderate Muslims and others whose orthodoxy was suspect were being gradually phased out. The champagne socialists were more or less completely discredited. It was the hour of the fundamentalists.

5

After Khomeini issued his edict in mid-February, non-Muslims routinely suggested that Muslims wanted to kill Rushdie because they couldn't argue with him. In fact, of course, Muslims can and indeed do argue—and argue well. The problem is that liberal guilt rarely lasts long enough for any of them to get a few pieces into the papers. In my own case, several interviews and features were pulled at the last moment as mysterious forces intervened. Editors of many important newspapers and periodicals resolutely rejected my contributions. So much for *our* freedom of speech.

Once the total veto on fundamentalist voices was broken, a new kind of restriction emerged. A statistical veto, in Saba Khalid's characteristically apt phrase, was imposed so that, say, for every dozen pieces strongly arguing against an Islamic stance, one piece arguing for an Islamic stance would slip through the net. Even so, Muslims weren't complaining because beggars can't be choosers.

At first all the editorials ritually rehearsed all the time-honoured prejudices about Muslims, particularly their alleged fanaticism. That intolerant creed which had once tried to ruin Europe was back again—this time as an apparently peaceful presence within the West, abetted by dark external forces and seconded by a financial network. The whole apparatus of prejudice had to be painstakingly dismantled during the Rushdie affair before anyone would even listen, let alone agree with the Muslim position. To be sure, there were prejudices in the Muslim camp too: the West is godless, passionless, faithless, corrupt to the bones. But there was little opportunity to voice these claims in the mainstream media. Besides, as we learn in the race relations industry, prejudice without power can safely be ignored.

Prejudices entertained by powerful groups and individuals cannot safely be ignored. Fortunately there came a time, after months of campaigning by Muslims, when, privately at least, many individuals, including a few newspaper editors and television programme makers, began to fear that they had misjudged the Muslims. Self-proclaimed defenders of freedom of speech as an absolute right began to see flaws in their arguments. Weren't there, after all, severe restrictions on such a freedom in common and statute law? What precisely was the rationale for curtailing the right to publish racist and obscene literature? A few pro-Rushdie writers and journalists have recently been busy distancing themselves from their own earlier derisory and dismissive comments made in the heat of the moment.

Bradford became a favourite shrine for repentant writers and journalists. A whole tribe of them have made the three hour journey from King's Cross to argue and debate in the city of the book-burners—devout Muhammadan chaps who speak English, read books, write books, and occasionally burn them. What has impressed them is that the long campaign by the Liberal Inquisition—its continuing intimidation—has not in any way stopped Muslims from protesting at the sacrilege of *The Satanic Verses*. Muslims have rightly condemned the regular use of double standards by Western commentators and the prejudicial rigour of their judgements against Muslims. Thus, for example, several non-Muslims have hinted that they would even defy any legal enactment according to which *The Satanic Verses* was banned. It is this kind of attitude and the excesses it has sanctioned which will be remembered for a long time. And the Muslims are not in a hurry to forget.

6

By early May 1989 two simple claims had been established beyond reasonable dispute: firstly, that Muslims of many shades of opinion had been genuinely and deeply offended by the contents of *The Satanic Verses* and, secondly, that freedom of speech was not absolute even in a liberal democratic society. But the issue was by no means resolved. While even liberal writers were happy to concede that some of Rushdie's allusions to the Koran were clearly blasphemous (in Muslim eyes), they did not interpret this to be *a* ground (let alone a *decisive* ground) for recommending a state ban. Both the deadlock and the apparent disagreement of principle behind it still remain and may indeed remain forever with us.

A substantial number of those concerned to defend the rights of Salman Rushdie have, even at this late hour, refused to concede that the Muslim outrage is authentic. There have been many attempts to attribute purely political or strategic motives to the Muslim campaigners. Indeed it has even been suggested, without any evidence at all, that Iran gave about a million dollars towards the costs of organising the anti-Rushdie demonstration in London on 27 May 1989. *The Economist* alleges that Saudi Arabia spent a quarter of a million pounds encouraging Bradford Muslims to protest even before the book-burning incident of mid-January. Maulana Abdal Husain Chaudhary of the Muslim Action Front (in London) and Sher Azam of the Bradford Council of Mosques both vehemently denied that external powers were funding British Muslim anger. In the case of Bradford at any rate, one look at the run-down state of the Council of Mosques premises is enough to remove doubts of Saudi funding.

'Who funds you?' is a cynical question intended to rob Muslims of their sincerity. Remember that it is, as David Caute points out, only the other side of the 'conspiracy coin': 'All this Rushdie business is a Western conspiracy!' is countered by 'All this Muslim outrage is due to Saudi funds!' In fact of course Islamic activities in Britain were not sustained by donations from foreign powers whether Arab states or Iran.

As soon as Muslims arrived in the United Kingdom in the late 1950s and early 1960s, long before the oil boom in the Arab world, they contributed towards the costs of provision of basic religious amenities, despite their poverty. Many houses were converted into simple places for prayer; none of the mosques, until recently, were grand works of architecture. Foreign donations did not help to initiate Islamic activities though some sustained them subsequently. To be sure, the British Muslim community is not without wealth. Even so, there is a striking contrast with Christian missions, funded by British and American voluntary bodies, currently operating in Muslim lands. There are vast donations to church personnel working among Muslims in Africa, the Middle East and Pakistan.

At the heart of these cynical allegations is the notion that Muslims remain Muslims for some reason extrinsic to their faith—such as foreign money. But the fact is that Islam has a powerful hold on the minds of Muslims in places as diverse as Britain and Iran. Whether this is due to the consummate indoctrination methods of the faith in early childhood or, more simply and credibly, a firm belief in its ultimate truth and sanity, can be left in the realm of reverent disagreement. Suffice it to say that even in China and Russia, Muslim conviction remains secure and powerful notwithstanding systematic Communist propaganda against Islam as a backward and regressive creed.

The point about the true motivation for being a Muslim is utterly central to any understanding of the profundity of the anger of the Muslim campaigners, and their determination. The overwhelming majority of Muslims have relentlessly argued against the sacrilege of Rushdie's book because they have sincerely felt outraged. This outrage has been spontaneous and universal and needs no foreign sponsors. Conscience suffices. This is not to deny that many Muslims have, as in Pakistan, exploited the Rushdie furore purely for their own personal political ends. But it is only charitable to concede that at least those who have been killed in the demonstrations were sincere in their indignation. Again, with respect to British Muslims, it may be possible to give many explanations for the depth of outrage: the psychic insecurity felt by poorer immigrants struggling to attain a sense of identity, the minority status of Muslims, external funding of the cause, and even a desire to impress each other and the non-Muslims. But it is helpful to include in this list the possibility that the outrage is authentic. After all, it is unwise to list every possible explanation other than the true one. Cynicism ought to have limits even in the Rushdie affair.

7

Martin Luther King's maxim may well serve to introduce our theme: 'Law does not change the heart—but it does restrain the heartless.' Every great tragedy teaches a truism; and the Rushdie affair is no exception. The freedom to express opinions on political and religious matters has to be restrained in the interests of social harmony. There are limits to freedom of speech even in liberal democracies; and there ought to be. For it is dangerous to allow motives of profit and sensationalism alone to determine the boundaries of public taste. We need the firm protection of the law to ensure that the interests of weaker individuals and groups are not substantially harmed by the irresponsible attitudes or actions of the more powerful individuals and groups in the same society. Accordingly, there are many legislative procedures for curtailing freedom of speech. For example, the Press Council and the laws of libel protect individuals' reputations from the extravagant claims of journalists and writers. Any juridical system that allows the famous to seek redress for libel cannot boast absolute freedoms of speech.

In the United Kingdom we have laws restricting by common consent many excesses in the freedom of expression. No one should deny the value of freedom of expression; and one of the problems we must accept in a multi-cultural society is the possibility of being routinely outraged. But the question here is about the *limits* of this outrage. According to English law, what is not prohibited is permitted; but many things are explicitly prohibited: blasphemy, obscenity, sedition, treason, incitement to racial hatred, breaches of national security, subversion, contempt of court and of Parliament, and libel. There are disputes, sometimes intractable, about the precise definition of the offences involved, but the underlying principles are universally accepted. Is it unreasonable to extend this concern to the prohibition of the publication of books like *The Satanic Verses* which are likely to inflame, through defamation, the feelings of a given section of society and, in doing so, to provoke public disorder? To be sure, prolonged public and parliamentary debate would together serve to establish the precise content of the law. But surely the moral concern behind the proposed legal enactment can readily be discerned and registered.

It is ironic that many in the present Conservative government should give lectures to their Muslim citizens about the virtues of freedom of speech. For we are living at a time of increased press censorship and routine political interference. We have for example the Official Secrets Act, the recent legal battle over *Spycatcher* and the continuing broadcasting difficulties over *Death on the Rock*. And who can ignore the formation of external watchdogs to police the media industry? The establishment of the British Standards Council is itself a sufficient indication of the government's desire to erode certain freedoms.

During the Rushdie affair, countless writers both in the West and in the Islamic world have been busy praising the virtues of freedom of speech and condemning the orthodox Muslim predilection towards censorship. Yet many professional writers would no doubt accept that one can abuse the privilege of freedom. In the international PEN charter of the world association of writers, the final sentence of the concluding paragraph reads: 'And since freedom implies voluntary restraint, members pledge themselves to oppose such evils of a free press as mendacious publication, deliberate falsehood and distortion of facts for political and personal ends.' Why can't Muslims appeal to this principle in their attempt to make a case against the publication of *The Satanic Verses*?

The liberal thinker Michael Ignatieff (*Observer*, 2 April 1989) has misleadingly argued that, at root, the disagreement between Muslims and their opponents is over 'incompatible conceptions of freedom, one in which freedom's limit is the sacred, one in which it is not'. Now, liberals certainly place the limit elsewhere— which is natural—since they reject the sacred. But the contrast, as Ignatieff wishes to interpret it, would be meaningful only if the opposite of the Islamic notion of freedom were virtual anarchy. And of course it isn't. Liberals do recognise the limits of freedom of speech; it would be odd if they drew the line at the sacred given that they reject the sacred. But, to men of faith, it may well seem arbitrary that the limits are drawn on the basis of race and gender.

Ignatieff argues, mistakenly, that behind this disagreement of principle lies another radical disagreement, namely, whether 'offence can be given to beliefs as such or merely to individuals'. Now, as it stands, this formulation of the issue seems incoherent. Can one attach any sense to Ignatieff's claim about offence being given to beliefs as such? Beliefs are not sentient creatures; consequently they are not capable of taking offence. Only people are offended in the required sense. Among the beliefs these people hold are beliefs about themselves and their universe—beliefs about race, gender and religious conviction. Laws never protect doctrines or beliefs as such against outrage. They protect the people who hold these beliefs against offence.

The point is not a quibble. Ignatieff tries to argue that, in a theocratic state like Iran, the law protects certain doctrines, while in allegedly free societies, like the United Kingdom, the law does not protect doctrines as such but rather protects individuals. It protects individuals through the application of laws of libel or laws against incitement to racial hatred. If so, Ignatieff has to reckon with the fact that the law of blasphemy remains on the statute books. This seems, on his understanding, an attempt to protect a doctrine rather than an individual. He dismisses it as a dead relic from a dead Christian past.

A Christian believer may wish to disagree. In any case, the issue remains. Ignatieff can dismiss it because he mis-identifies it. The issue is not whether one should protect individuals rather than beliefs. For it is incoherent to protect beliefs as such unless there are people who hold them and who might be offended by an attack on them. In one sense, one has no choice but to protect people, as opposed to their beliefs. It is both possible and necessary to protect beliefs because people's sensibilities are at stake. The real reason for Ignatieff's rejection of the blasphemy law is not that it protects doctrines as opposed to individuals but because it recognises that religious conviction can be as relevant a consideration as race and gender in the formulation of legal restraint.

Religion is, for Muslims, as much a part of their essential self-definition as race or gender. There is a sense in which one cannot escape one's race or, arguably, gender. But for the overwhelming majority of Muslims, religion is also an inescapable fact of one's nature. So, the stock liberal argument fails. It is not as though one could simply discard one religious conviction for another or even for none at all. For many Muslims, Islam is a part of their being from the cradle to the grave. Such a feature cannot reasonably be seen as being peripheral or incidental to one's self-image.

This is not an argument primarily for protecting ideas against abuse — in any case, as I have shown, an incoherent proposal. It is an argument for protecting the collective dignity of those groups — such as Muslims and Sikhs — whose members, rightly or wrongly, do define their own ideals or the worth of their lives in terms of irreducibly religious notions.

8

'Freedom is not a holy belief, nor even a supreme value.' So writes Michael Ignatieff in the *Observer* of 2 April 1989. It is, he tells us, a contestable concept. Is it? To be sure, liberal thinkers would argue that all the central concepts of modern secular political theory are essentially contestable. Freedom, rights, power, democracy itself. Yet the behaviour of apolo-gists for liberalism during the Rushdie affair gives the lie to the claim that they interpret freedom to be a negotiable value.

It is an axiom of democratic thought that the truth about the political world is not ascertainable in a final or absolute way, and that all men and women are fallible, not least those in positions of power and influence. Accordingly, individuals and groups with conflicting interests should properly discuss and negotiate solutions on the basis of enlightened self-interest. But there has been little evidence of any such reasoning during the Rushdie affair. The notion of negotiating with these uncivilised Muslims has been dogmatically rejected. It has indeed been a case of our light and sagacity versus their darkness and obscurantism.

It is the Muslims who have wished to remind liberals that freedom is indeed a contestable concept. The Muslims have plausibly argued that the issue is not the right to censure the Islamic tradition, for that right exists and is routinely exercised. The issue is whether or not any civilised society should tolerate, let alone encourage, writers to ridicule and mock the convictions of a major world constituency. Does the secular clergy have the right to canonise freedom of speech as an absolute value overriding all other relevant considerations?

The liberal fundamentalists have betrayed themselves. For the central principle of secular liberalism is that difference in ideological posture among groups and individuals should rarely, if ever, entail a restriction of human sympathies. Yet the Muslims were pilloried for defending their dignity as believers.

It is significant that the British Muslims' rebellion, with all its impotence (only the powerless burn books and demonstrate on the streets), has elicited anger rather than sympathy. Could it be that Islam challenges the moral absolutism of the liberal establishment setting itself up as the sole cultural overseer and arbiter of public taste and value? Even a purely rhetorical protest by the British Muslims has galvanised the opposition; everyone has gathered together to warm themselves by the fire of Western passion. Where is the negotiated compromise, the judicious pragmatism of a liberal democratic culture committed to rejecting authoritarian dictates and the passionate arrogance authoritarianism allegedly engenders? After the Rushdie episode, it is even harder to endorse a faith in the humility of secular liberal postures of power.

The point is hugely significant. Islam is a salutary reminder of the need for political humility in secular statecraft. It is always a routine assumption of Western political theory that the possibilities of political humility are exhausted by purely secular postures of power. Yet the assumption is questionable. For it is secular statecraft, not theocracy, that gave us Hiroshima and two 'World' (or rather European) Wars. Some of the most incisive critiques of the abuse of power have come from the pen of those troubled by the hubris of secularity when it rejects any liability to forces greater than itself. With so much talk of The Thought Police and Muslim fundamentalists in the same breath, it is well to remember that Orwell's political masterpiece *1984* is a critique of totalitarianism in secular dress. Big Brother was not an Ayatollah, not even an ordinary Muslim. The Liberal Inquisition has its Thought Police too.

9

Freedom is more holy to liberals than Michael Ignatieff would have us believe. In fact, liberal society too holds certain shibboleths beyond rational debate. Some things do matter; and principles cannot be weighed in the scales of pragmatism or diplomacy. Yet if freedom of speech is a sacred or otherwise unnegotiable value for the liberal West, why shouldn't the question of Muhammad's honour have a similar status for Muslim believers?

It is fashionable for Western writers to pretend to be suspicious of all apologias and enthusiasms. Yet aren't we all apologists for one belief or another—if only the true one? Nor will it do to pretend, as some might neatly think, 'But truth needs no apology'. For that would only be true in a world in which truth were both manifest and men were honest. But, in the contemporary universe, truth is extremely hard to come by and, even when attained, there is no shortage of those professionally engaged in obscuring it.

The Rushdie affair is, in the last analysis, admittedly about
fanaticism on behalf of God. Immediately we need to be
cautious. For fanaticism is by no means the monopoly of the
Muslim fundamentalists. Indeed fanaticism is often merely
other folks' passion. Nations can be fanatical about trivial
matters (such as football and sensuality) or elevated matters
(such as religion and morality). Could it be, then, that we
can all live with some prejudices but not with others?

The Archbishop of York wrote in a letter to *The Times* (1
March 1989) that abolishing the law of blasphemy would
indicate 'that in the last resort our society holds nothing
sacred, apart from the freedom of writers to write what they
like. This is, for obvious reasons, attractive to
writers . . . [but] why should it have absolute priority over
all other claims to sacredness?' Fair question, surely; and one
not to be answered by evasive liberal rhetoric about religious
intolerance being particularly oppressive. Intolerance, no
matter what its source, leads to oppression and denial of
human rights. It is a prejudice, if a pardonable one, to think
that the intolerance of those who make particularly loud professions of tolerance is to be preferred to the intolerance of
those who don't.

10

Neither conspiracy nor passion has been lacking in the Rushdie affair. One of Viking Penguin's own editorial advisers,
Khuswant Singh, wisely counselled against the publication of
The Satanic Verses. Certainly one can have conspiracies in
the strong sense of actually having influential people in
smoke-filled rooms whispering sinister secrets. A society as
complex as ours doesn't normally work like that. But conspiracies in the weaker sense abound. There has been a systematic attempt, both before and during the Rushdie affair,
to exclude the broadcasting of well-argued and convincing
Muslim contentions.

After seeing *The Late Show* on 8 May 1989 on BBC2,
the historian David Caute wrote to me: 'Isn't it time they

despatched you to interview the liberal intellectuals in their "belljars"?' It was high time indeed. But even to have got this far, I privately mused, was an achievement. It would be at least another fifty years before Ignatieff and Akhtar could reverse roles. And that not simply because Akhtar had a brown skin. After all, Salman Rushdie and Tariq Ali also have brown skins. But Akhtar and his ilk happen to believe in that dangerous creed—Islam—at once too far from and yet too close to the Western conscience. Fifty years does not seem to me to be too generous an estimate.

Nor has passion been in short supply during the Rushdie affair. Yasmin Ali is wrong when she claims that the reaction from the liberal left has been 'depressingly bloodless' in comparison with 'the militant wrath of Shabbir Akhtar and others' (*New Statesman and Society*, 16 March 1989). What is true is that the passion from the liberal camp has been reactionary and secondary: there has been a passionate reservation about the passion of Muslims.

For all their claims to objectivity, the views of most liberal commentators bear clearly on them the imprint of partisan enthusiasm and ethnocentric loyalty. Thus, for example, Fay Weldon has recently canonised Rushdie! Given that St Salman's incoherent fantasy appears to have fooled the West, at least the miracle-working requirement for canonisation has been fulfilled.

The fact is of course that *The Satanic Verses* is a mediocre piece of literature the popularity of which among people who know nothing about Islam invites one to look at their motives. The Western literary establishment has inflated the book into a major cultural phenomenon in a decade that must show some claim to significance before it ends.

It has been a long summer of persecution. In the end, there will be, as usual in the aftermath of English obstinacy, a compromise solution embedded in insincere apologies, from all sides, for past excesses. But any hasty militancy, by the Muslims, would be a great tragedy for Islam. For it would give the liberal establishment a martyr they badly need and don't deserve. Those who regularly mistake fashion for passion, and pray that others do so too, cannot have the right to any tremendous cause, whether for Islam or against it.

4 From Teheran with Love

'I inform the proud Muslim people of the world that the author of the "Satanic Verses" book, which is against Islam, the Prophet and the Koran, and all those involved in its publication who were aware of its content, are sentenced to death. I ask all the Muslims to execute them wherever they find them.'

Ayatollah Khomeini's edict, issued on St Valentine's day, certainly seemed no message of love. It shocked audiences world-wide. For most non-Muslims it merely confirmed, if such confirmation were needed, the all-pervasive fanaticism and intolerance of 'fundamentalist' Islam. Khomeini had become one of the many violent witnesses to the bigotry and anti-intellectualism of the Muslim faith. In a long line of totalitarian leaders, he was unwilling to tolerate the diversity of opinion all traditions naturally spawn over the centuries.

Many Muslims, however, applauded Khomeini as a hero. Members of both major sects, Shia'h and Sunni, were united in their praise for his stance. In sharp contrast to the deafening silence in the Arab heartland of Islam, at least he had spoken. And spoken clearly. Had he not stood up for the honour of Muhammad—the noble messenger of God? Wasn't this proof of his love for God? Many Muslims privately thought that Khomeini had got the date right after all.

1

'Publish and be damned' was never truer than in Salman Rushdie's case. But it can be fun being published—and merely being damned for it. Before the religious edict (*fatwa*) from the Iranian cleric, Rushdie and his publishers had been having a good time at the expense of the powerless and voiceless Muslim masses. Even the desperate book-burning (in Bradford a month earlier in mid-January 1989) had not seriously worried them. After all, as many in the press would have us believe, these Muhammadan peasants are not capable of appreciating great works of fiction. At any rate, a relatively incomprehensible piece of literature weighing in at about a quarter of a million words, was transformed into an instant bestseller. It was every author's dream. In repeated television appearances, Rushdie enjoyed being represented as the great liberal freethinker, dedicated to progress and enlightenment, harassed by a narrow-minded and narrow-hearted 'fundamentalist' minority among the Muslims.

'Publish and be damned' is a Western slogan; 'Publish and be hanged' is Khomeini's version. Rushdie was destined to pay a high price for what was, in Muslim eyes, very obvious literary impudence. In Teheran, the controversy surrounding *The Satanic Verses* had been monitored by the Ayatollah's advisers since October 1988. But no action had been recommended. Iran's chargé d'affaires, Akhundzadeh Basti, was in London throughout the months preceding the delivery of the *fatwa* and must surely have advised his government on the developments in Britain. But it was the riots in Islamabad that were to supply the last straw. Iranian television reported that half-a-dozen people had been killed in anti-Rushdie demonstrations in the Pakistani capital on 12 February 1989, with one more civilian death a day later in neighbouring Kashmir. Khomeini asked for a full report on *The Satanic Verses*; a day later he pronounced his famous *fatwa* according to his interpretation of Islamic law. Within hours there was talk of a price on Rushdie's head. This was indeed, as V. S. Naipaul remarked in an interview in Calcutta, 'an extreme form of literary criticism'.

2

Western condemnation of Khomeini's *fatwa* was hasty, loud, clear and unanimous. Commentators in the media saw it as the Muslims' collective regression into the fanatical intolerance of the medieval era—or, I suppose, of the more recent days of the American Wild West. Many writers speculated that it was difficult even to explain, let alone justify, the ferocity of Khomeini's reaction. Could it be that he had interpreted Rushdie's book as a personal attack on the Imam 'bent on rolling back history itself', setting his face against progress and justice?

At any rate, virtually all Western writers, particularly British, French and American ones, jointly condemned the *fatwa* as failing to meet Western ethical requirements. It was brutal and unjust. Such 'remote control' assassinations smacked more of the Mafia than of a civilised state.

There were over-reactions too. The normally moderate if passionate Nobel Prize winner, Elie Wiesel said: 'If the death threat succeeds in silencing the Indian born author, it would mean not only the end of literature but the end of civilisation.' An exaggeration surely; civilisation may well survive without Salman Rushdie and his works.

Muslim, particularly Iranian, reaction was no less passionate. Khomeini's *fatwa* and the price placed on Rushdie's head was, it was argued, no different from the bounty offered for bank robbers in the American Wild West during the nineteenth century. Was the sheriff then a murderer because he offered a reward for the criminal caught dead or alive? Nor will it do to retort, urged the Iranians, that the alleged crime in Rushdie's case was not committed within a territory under the jurisdiction of the Iranian state. There were, the Iranians pointed out somewhat weakly, instances of one nation's authorities sentencing a citizen of another country: the British government once sentenced a future Israeli Prime Minister, Mr Begin, *in absentia*, for involvement in Palestinian terrorism in the 1940s.

The Western outrage is the result of double standards. For, after all, surreptitious violence in the pursuit of such goals as national and ideological security as well as alleged anti-terrorism is morally acceptable to many European and American critics of Khomeini. Are there no Western heads of state who occasionally condone the taking, albeit secretly, even of innocent life in the pursuit of aims like security and world peace? Perhaps it is Khomeini's candour, with its published

flavour of Machiavellianism, that offends the Western conscience. At any rate, it is wise to resist the obvious conclusion
that Iranian interpretations of Islam necessarily patronise
brutality more than other ideologies do.

It is in general unwise for assassins to publish their inten-
tions to their would-be victims. Given the frankness of Khomeini's orders, it is difficult to believe that Khomeini was inter-
ested in having Rushdie assassinated. (Indeed, in a
paradoxical way, the *fatwa* saved Rushdie's life: the tight
security surrounding him, in the wake of the Iranian threat,
has made it difficult for outraged Muslim individuals even in
Britain to harm him.) Khomeini himself probably reasoned
that an individual keenly threatened with death suffers far
more than one who is killed without warning.

'Be careful with Muhammad', warns the slogan. Rushdie
must have known it. Anyone born within the Realm of Islam
is bound to know it. Indeed, many outsiders are well aware
of the Muslim tendency to take religious conviction seriously.
There is ample evidence in Islamic history for the view that
Muslims hold their Prophet in great esteem. At any rate,
Rushdie's literary terrorism had been answered by Khomeini's threat of physical terrorism.

3

Sir Geoffrey Howe of the United Kingdom was among the
first Western leaders to condemn Khomeini's *fatwa*. Within
days of Khomeini's declaration, Howe had elicited the unconditional support of the European and American communities.
To show solidarity with the British decision to withdraw British diplomats from Teheran, the EEC (European Economic
Community) countries decided on 20 February to withdraw
their diplomats too. The newly elected President George
Bush also joined in the Western criticism of Iran's leader as
a tyrant and murderer.

In Teheran, the initial reaction was one of sincere surprise.
Why had Britain over-reacted on the Rushdie issue? After
all, Britain had taken the initiative in normalising diplomatic

relations with Iran; indeed the British Embassy had been reopened in November 1988.

Iran immediately responded to the EEC reaction by an equally dramatic move. All Iranian diplomats in Europe were recalled. Muslims in many European cities marched, raising pro-Iranian slogans like 'Khomeini—the honour of Islam'. On 22 February an ageing Ayatollah Khomeini issued a statement. The unprecedented reaction shown against Iran, he declared, was due to the West's alarm at the potential power of Islam. It was this threat to Western hegemony, Khomeini argued, that could alone explain the sheer ferocity of Western indignation. The reaction of European and American governments had little to do with defending the rights of a black individual and more to do with their frustration at having been denied an opportunity to ridicule Islam. Even the presence of one truly Islamic state, Khomeini concluded, could put considerable limits on the power of non-Muslims to insult the Muslims.

One day after Khomeini's reaction to the Western outrage, the Iranian Parliament and Assembly of Experts tabled a motion asking the government to break off diplomatic relations with the United Kingdom. The Iranians suggested that, given Britain's past record of ideological enmity towards Muslims, the British government must publicly condemn *The Satanic Verses* and apologise to the Muslim community for injury to feelings. Meanwhile, many religionists throughout the Islamic world were coming out in favour of Khomeini's edict. On 25 February Indian police shot dead about a dozen more Muslim demonstrators in Rushdie's native Bombay. The Imam of India's Jami'a Mosque in Delhi openly supported Khomeini's *fatwa*. Another leading Indian Muslim religionist, Maulana Hasan Ali Nadawi, no friend of Khomeini's and indeed passionately opposed to Shia'h Islam, endorsed the Iranian cleric's judgement as 'just and appropriate'. The Mufti of Jerusalem's al-Aqsa Mosque concurred. In the Lebanon the powerful Sheikh Shaban, leader of the Tauhid Movement, came out in favour of the *fatwa*, praising Khomeini as a courageous Muslim soldier opposing a 'Zionist plot against Islam'.

At the end of February the Iranian Parliament passed a motion giving the United Kingdom seven days to impose a ban on Rushdie's book and apologise. Iran's chargé d'affaires, Akhundzadeh Basti, left London for Teheran. He supported Khomeini's *fatwa* as a 'divine order' which no one could change. The whole aim of the Islamic Revolution, he told reporters just before his departure, was to defend Islam throughout the world.

While Western diplomatic pressure against Iran was increasing, there were many more demonstrations in which Muslims condemned Rushdie as well as the British government. Throughout the Muslim world and indeed Europe and the United States, outraged Muslims took to the streets in a rare show of unity. British and American flags were burnt and the embassies stoned. Arab governments, particularly the Saudis, were condemned for their silence over the Anglo-Rushdie scandal; they were passionately accused of being co-conspirators with the West in a plot to destroy Islam. Khomeini, by contrast, emerged as the isolated but celebrated hero who had saved Islam in the hour of trial. Muslims the world over were deeply impressed by the courageous stance of the Iranians given that they had already paid such a high price for their defence of Islamic values.

The one week's notice given to the British government by the Iranians was due to end on 7 March. Iran cancelled a technical exhibition, scheduled for 5 March in Teheran, involving 50 British firms. On 2 March the Labour MP for Bradford West, Max Madden, urged Parliament to act quickly to resolve the Rushdie affair. He warned that unless the British government tried to satisfy the demands of its own Muslim citizens, Khomeini could not be isolated as an outsider agitating the Muslims settled in the United Kingdom. On the same day, Geoffrey Howe and Margaret Thatcher both acknowledged that *The Satanic Verses* was indeed offensive and sympathised with Muslim outrage. But neither agreed to consider Muslim demands for a state ban on the book. Many parts of *The Satanic Verses*, argued Geoffrey Howe, also provocatively compared Britain with Hitler's Fascist Germany. And while that offended him and his colleagues, it was not a sufficient reason for banning the book. Freedom of speech was, he continued, a British tradition that had to be defended at all costs. Diplomatic relations between Iran and the United Kingdom were officially severed on 7 March.

4

We shall in due course examine Khomeini's *fatwa* in the context of the British Muslim stance and indeed the reactions of other Muslims world-wide. But it is wise at this stage to survey briefly the traditional Islamic beliefs and laws about blasphemy, apostasy and treason.

All sacred literature in the Hebrew-Christian and Islamic traditions makes references to blasphemy, apostasy, and heresy. Let us begin with blasphemy. The Old Testament (Leviticus 24:16) prescribes corporal punishment for blasphemy, while the New Testament (Matthew 12:32) is content to warn that blasphemy is unforgivable in both worlds. Justinian prescribed the death penalty for blasphemy; it became part of the codification of Roman law in AD 535. In later and medieval Christianity, both Protestant and Catholic, blasphemy remained punishable by death. Indeed blasphemy is still a criminal offence in the United Kingdom though it does not figure in the legal systems of many other European countries.

It is fair to add that blasphemy can be a meaningful offence both in a pious and a secular context. For secular nations that were formerly Christian, 'blasphemy' would imply the use of grossly outrageous language concerning one's own nation or some inviolable ideal of that nation. In parts of the United States, there is still a civil penalty on the books for any extreme outrage against the flag.

In the Islamic tradition too it is possible to blaspheme against God, his revealed message and his Prophet. Surprisingly, however, the Koran does not legislate a penalty for such blasphemy. Chapter 4 (verse 151) refers to Jewish blasphemy against Mary, the mother of Christ. But no punishment, other than a spiritual one (in terms of divine wrath) is mentioned.

Similarly, the Koran frequently accuses the Christians of committing blasphemy against God (or, more strictly, one of the names of God since the person of God is too exalted for any indignity to reach him). Once again, no penalty is prescribed. Indeed far from legislating punishment here, the Koran discourages Muslims even from verbally abusing the deities of idolaters and blasphemers: 'And revile not those whom they call upon God, lest they, out of spite, revile [the true] God in their ignorance' (6:109).

Things are somewhat different when a believing Muslim is thought to blaspheme against God or his messenger. The Koran itself makes no clear reference to such a scenario. Subsequent learned opinion has always remained divided but there is no shortage of those prescribing imprisonment or even execution for heretics and individuals thought to have committed offences against the dignity of God or his messenger. Such measures have rarely been carried out, official Islam having always been relatively tolerant of heresy. But there are famous exceptions. The tenth-century mystic-saint Mansur al-Hallaj had, in a moment of ecstasy, exclaimed 'I am the truth', effectively identifying himself with the Deity. He was executed by an outraged orthodoxy eager to avenge blasphemy against the divine name.

The problems of identifying apostasy and the determination of appropriate punitive measures are both large and controversial. By and large, the Koran prescribes penalties for what may be termed 'social' crimes — such as adultery, fornication, theft, highway robbery, causing public disorder — as opposed to purely personal or spiritual offences such as hypocrisy, dishonesty in interpersonal relationships, back-biting, financial malpractice, lapse from strict Islamic piety, and private loss of faith. As I understand it, the sacred scripture of Islam does not prescribe any penalty in this world for apostasy alone. It condemns those who 'turn their backs on guidance' as sinning against God; the works of renegades are in vain and Hell is often said to be their destination (2:217). However, apostasy is punishable by death if it is aggravated, variously, by treachery in a military context, a breach of contract or treaty with a Muslim party to an agreement, ideological or

physical enmity to Muslims or the Islamic state, any attempt
to bring the religion of Islam into serious disrepute in the
eyes of rejectors, and related offences.

Given that the infant Islamic state in Medina could easily
be infiltrated and subsequently destroyed by external political
forces working in alliance with fellow conspirators within, the
sacred volume has much to say on recantation and apostasy
as well as heresy, temporary belief feigned by individuals
trying to create confusion among believers, and undetectable
varieties of hypocrisy. There are ten references to recantation
and scores of references, including a whole chapter, to hypocrisy. Neither hypocrisy nor recantation merit corporal punishment. In fact, according to the Koran itself, neither merit any
penalty at all in this world. Thus, for example, three Jews in
Medina who recanted according to Chapter 3 (v.72), did so
with complete impunity. Indeed, Chapter 5 (v.54) speaks of
collective apostasy by an entire generation of Muslim
believers. No worldly punishment is prescribed; God simply
promises to raise a generation more worthy of the faith.

A virtually conclusive argument against the death penalty
for recantation from Islam is implied in the Koran's famous
chapter concerning 'Women' (v.137). 'Those who believe,
then disbelieve, then believe again, then disbelieve and then
increase in their disbelief, such are those whom God will
never forgive nor guide to the path.' But a renegade could
hardly enjoy the benefit of repeated belief and disbelief if
capital punishment were prescribed for the initial act of apostasy. To be sure, this verse could be interpreted alternatively
to be simply a commentary on the limits of repentance and
divine forgiveness. But such a reading does not preclude the
more obvious interpretation that even repeated apostasy, let
alone apostasy, is not punishable by death.

Recantation of itself, then, does not seem to warrant the
death penalty. This interpretation of the Koran is supported
by the Prophet's own political dealings. We have a list of more
or less all individuals who were considered to be dangerous to
the Islamic state at the time of Muhammad's triumphant re-
entry into Mecca. Though a number were executed, none of
these was executed for committing apostasy. But the Koran,

the prophetic example, and all five schools of law (four Sunni, one Shia'h) are unanimous in their endorsement of capital punishment for public recantation coupled with active opposition to the House of Islam.

Private recantation from Islam aggravated by disobedience to Islamic law or physical violence against Muslim lives and property always warrants the 'extreme' (*hudood*) punishments. Thus, for example, immediately after the death of the Prophet, the First Caliph took military action against certain tribes which had relapsed into their previous paganism. But the rebel tribes were not only committing apostasy; they were also refusing to pay the obligatory alms-tax due to the infant Islamic state. In effect the tribes were breaking their pledge to the Islamic authorities. Such apostasy, coupled with a breach of contract, effectively amounted to treason against the Islamic state; and the death penalty was accordingly invoked against the rebel tribes.

Given that the Koran famously makes no distinction between religious and political authority, many Muslim scholars of law from the earliest times have considered recantation to be not merely sinful but also an act of high treason against the Islamic state. Capital punishment has therefore sometimes been demanded even for privately committed apostasy. The major aims have been to safeguard against opportunist conversions and to prevent the entry of spies into the Muslim community. Clearly, if people entering the household of Islam know there is no way out, only those sincerely inclined to accept Islam are likely to enter at all. There have been many cases of individuals converting to Islam and then relapsing into their original faith once privileged access to required information had been obtained or certain attractive worldly privileges—such as polygamy and the facility of divorce—had been enjoyed. Only those suspected of spying are likely to face execution primarily for broadly political (as opposed to religious) considerations of security and the public interest. But there are jurists who wish to block all apostasy in order to avoid any abuse of the privileges Islam offers to its adherents.

The death penalty for apostasy has been demanded in recent decades, for some of the reasons mentioned above, by several learned authorities such as Sheikh Abu Zahra of Egypt and Maulana Abul Ala Maududi of Pakistan. The general view here is that conversion is a one-way traffic. While converts to Islam are welcome, any leakage from the vessel of faith cannot be tolerated. Male apostates are to be executed unless they are mentally disturbed or below the age of consent (normally set at twelve), or congenitally and invincibly ignorant of the truth of the Islamic religion or converted forcibly to Islam from the revealed faiths of Judaism and Christianity. Female apostates, with the same exceptions as above, are treated more leniently: indefinite incarceration until recantation. All apostates, male or female, are allowed a period of grace in which they can recant and repent of their decision.

Although many contemporary learned authorities reject the view that apostasy is a capital offence, there are religionists, particularly in India, Pakistan, Bangladesh, and Iran, who would opt for capital punishment. The view is that those born in the House of Islam cannot leave the realm of faith without bringing disgrace on the family of the apostate. Typically, the law of Islam rarely needs to be applied in such cases since the apostate's family will take the law into its own hands and kill the apostate on account of the stigma thought to attach to the rest of the family. Particularly in Indian sub-continental contexts, a man's *izzat* (roughly speaking, honour) is thought to be at stake if a family member converts to another faith. There is immense social pressure to disown the apostate if not to kill him or her. In Birmingham recently a Bengali father murdered his own daughter because she left Islam to become a Jehovah's Witness.

Among jurists favouring capital punishment for recantation, the definition of Muslim is so broad as to include any individual calling himself or herself a Muslim, no matter how he or she behaves. This was the definition used at the time of the first census in Medina during the Prophet's rule. Ever since, it has been considered both a necessary and a sufficient condition for being a Muslim that one publicly affirms that one is a Muslim—normally by reciting the creed: 'There is no god except God and Muhammad is his envoy.' After that no one has the right to question the Muslim status of the speaker. The practice of Islam has never been taken to be a condition of being a Muslim; many Muslims fail to fulfil their normal religious obligations. Those Muslims who break the laws of Islam are appropriately punished but their status as Muslim believers does not depend on the propriety of their conduct. Such individuals may be seen (and often see themselves) as bad Muslims; but bad believers are believers none the less. And God alone is the final judge in matters of the faith. The Koran nowhere restricts entry into Paradise to good Muslims (or indeed even to Muslims as opposed to Jews and Christians).

From a community confident of his wisdom, the Prophet routinely received requests to single out the lukewarm and hypocritical elements from the truly faithful ones. He declined and thereby set a precedent for all future Muslim attempts to judge what is in other people's hearts. We know on the authority of ibn Ishaq that in the raid led by Ghalib bin Abdullah al-Kalbi, a man was killed by Usama bin Zayd and his companion, despite his confession of faith at the time of capture. Asked by the Prophet about the killing, Zayd replied that the captured man had become a Muslim out of fear. The commentator Ahmad ibn Hanbal adds that the Prophet angrily asked Usama bin Zayd whether or not he had opened the victim's heart to check the authenticity of his confession. With such incidents in mind, Muslim jurists have usually agreed to give the benefit of the doubt to the suspected hypocrite or apostate. As the standard Islamic theological maxim has it: 'It is better to be mistaken in forgiveness than in punishment.'

There is currently no consensus among Islam's religious intelligentsia in Cairo's seminary al-Azhar regarding the correct attitude towards apostasy. But the Draconian rulings of some earlier religionists favouring capital punishment have not, in general, found favour with the contemporary Egyptian authorities at the Sunni world's policy-making centre. In practice of course the majority of people born in the House of Islam, who wish to avoid fulfilling the requirements of Islamic piety, can do so with impunity. There is, if you like, practical apostasy all the time. By and large, Muslims who privately commit apostasy are not harassed by the Islamic establishment. However, those who publicly insult the Prophet or launch abusive attacks on the contents of the Koran and the derivative Islamic tradition are almost always taken to task for it.

Enlightened Muslim opinion now recognises that, within the modern community of Islamic peoples, there is a significant number of individuals who are its members by chance rather than by choice. There is therefore a high price to be paid for keeping the entire community in line with any unduly harsh policy or ruling on apostasy. For it would breed hypocrisy; and disaffected hypocrites have always been a source of treason and sedition even in Muhammad's own day. Lukewarm and time-serving allegiances, ultimately disruptive of the social fabric, are hardly worth the price.

To be sure, a missionary faith like Islam cannot turn a blind eye on the heretic or the apostate—'the brother that walketh disorderly' in St Paul's idiom (2 Thessalonians 3:6). And Muslims certainly don't turn a blind eye. The persecution of the Ahmadi sect in Pakistan (which has been expelled from the House of Islam) is a sufficient witness to that. For the ordinary Muslim, meeting an apostate is a far more dramatically disturbing experience than meeting a Jew or a Christian.

These related fears of heresy, apostasy and social dismemberment, however, have to be set in the balance with a due regard for freedom of belief. The potential risks of heresy and apostasy inherent in the offer of religious freedom are, it seems to me, worth taking. For one thing, if there is a God, it can be safely assumed that he wants a voluntary response born of genuine conviction, rooted in reflection and morally responsible choice. Seen in this light, heresy and apostasy are morally more acceptable than any hypocritical attachment to orthodox opinion out of the fear of public sanctions.

Nor is this a position devoid of traditional religious support. Scriptural passages are to hand favouring such a stance: 'There should be no compulsion in religion' (2:256). Conscientious disbelief has to be tolerated. A verse, revealed during the early Meccan ministry of the Prophet, addressed to idolaters, may well serve as part of a specifically Islamic manifesto on freedom of conscience and conviction: 'To you your religion, to me mine' (109:6).

5

'The only reward of those who make war upon God and His Messenger and strive to create disorder in the land', reads chapter 5 (vv.33–4) of the Koran, 'will be that they will be killed or crucified, or have their hands and feet on alternate sides cut off, or will be exiled from the land. Such will be their humiliation in this world, and in the world yet to come there awaits them an awful doom. This is so except in the case of those who repent before you overpower them. For God is forgiving, merciful.' Rushdie is charged, under the provisions of the law derived from these verses, with creating *fasad* (public disorder) in a land under divine sovereignty.

Khomeini's *fatwa*, like the varied edicts issued by other jurists in the Islamic world, does not by and large hinge on the fact that Rushdie is an apostate or a blasphemer or indeed even a *shatim* – an individual who insults any messenger of God, whether Muhammad or his prophetic predecessors. (The penalty for a *shatim*, unlike a blasphemer or an apostate, is irrevocable.) The author of *The Satanic Verses* is charged with causing *fasad* or corruption in the world. In Rushdie's case, his privately committed apostasy is thought to be aggravated by a public declaration of ideological enmity against the Realm of Islam. Given that, in Islamic thought, no distinction obtains between religious and political crimes, Rushdie's attack on the religion of Islam is interpreted to be an act of high treason against the Islamic state. Now, as it happens, the underlying charge of *fasad* can be levelled indifferently at Muslims and non-Muslims alike, whether within or outside the House of Islam; hence Khomeini's decision to include, within the remit of his *fatwa*, Rushdie's non-Muslim accomplices, namely, his publishers and related parties.

It is important to understand the exact nature of Rushdie's crime. He is charged, under the regulations of chapter 5 of the Koran, with a declaration of 'war upon God and His

77

Messenger' and, in doing so, with creating 'corruption (*fasad*) in the land'. For Rushdie has been an apostate—an atheist in his case—for many years before the publication of *The Satanic Verses*. Many Muslims have known this and few have even criticised him, let alone threatened his life. Rushdie is in good company. Many other writers, journalists, poets, thinkers and artists from a similar background also repudiated Islam as a false religion. It is a well-known fact that almost all of the Third World socialists resident in the West have, in their eagerness to disown their roots and origins, sought to cauterise Islam from their hearts and 'souls'. Indeed many have, in addition, engaged in a militant campaign against the faith of their forebears—though usually from the safety of a flat in London or Paris.

Rushdie's secular lifestyle, then, has been tolerated by Muslims. No one has denied him the right, as an imaginative writer, to take legitimate liberties with his own sacred heritage. But liberty is not licence; and most of us would think at least twice before defaming the character of a man whose life and work have been, rightly or wrongly, held in esteem for 1500 years by a major constituency of the human race. Nor is the ground for such caution merely fear of the Muslim reaction. One has some obligation to be fair in one's criticisms and reservations even about—especially about—outlooks one conscientiously rejects.

Rushdie is entitled to reject Islam or indeed to reinterpret, in an idiosyncratic way, some of its doctrines and regulations. But this is largely a matter of private option; any public declarations should be made in conscious awareness of the risks. An authorship, no matter how personal in its formation or motivation, can hardly remain private in its consequences. And self-censorship is a meaningful demand in a world of varied and passionately held convictions. What Rushdie publishes about Islam is not just his business. It is everyone's— at least every Muslim's—business.

Rushdie is not a newcomer to controversy and even to book-bannings. Indeed he has in the past, through the medium of fiction, ably criticised influential Muslims. All societies, alive to the pressures of the contemporary world, must allow such critiques on pain of becoming repressive and outdated. And Rushdie's earlier work *Shame* caused deep offence to some individuals in the Pakistani government, though it did not arouse the spontaneous anger and universal outrage occasioned by *The Satanic Verses*.

The reason for the different reactions to the two novels is of central significance. To criticise or even to prostitute the reputations of individuals who profess the Islamic creed is one thing; reviling things sacred is quite another. To accuse and to be the subject of accusation are altogether human; both are a part of the failings of our common humanity. Muslims are no exception here. But while matters of private injury to feeling are within the province of the discretion and forgiveness of individuals, offences against the dignity of God and His Messenger may well seem inexcusable acts of gross immorality. Nor should one dismiss the latter claim as merely a fanatical judgement harboured in a religious enthusiasm that is admittedly alien to the secular West. If we are to understand people, including the Muslims, we cannot begin by ignoring the factors and perceptions that inform their outlook, that are a part of their make-up.

Many writers, including Rushdie in his earlier work, disguise their hatred of Muhammad and Islam by pretending that their only target is the intolerance and fanaticism of the mullahs and clerics. In *The Satanic Verses* Rushdie courageously takes one step further, realising, quite rightly, that one cannot indefinitely hate Muslims without also hating the faith and the prophetic pattern they love. Accordingly, he makes explicit his reservations about Islam and his animosity towards the Arabian Prophet. Rushdie no longer pretends that he is merely concerned to condemn a few 'fundamentalists' (like Khomeini). He goes to the heart of the matter. He cuts Allah down to size and puts Muhammad in his place. It cannot be expected that Muslims should fail to react to such an ideological challenge.

6

The Rushdie affair comes at a time of sharply opposed and competing trends in the Arab, and more broadly, Muslim world. Though there are countless signs of religious revival— and Western talk of 'radical Islamic fundamentalism' is not entirely without basis—there co-exist passionate commitments to secularity. Indeed there are many in the contemporary Muslim world who remain, in Jalal al-e-Ahmad's phrase, 'Westoxicated'. Not every Muslim has sobered up under the influence of Khomeini's Islamic revolution.

There are roughly fifty Muslim states today (if we include Nigeria, India and Uganda) and Muslims in all of them have reacted, in different ways, both to the publication of *The Satanic Verses* and to the *fatwa* of Ayatollah Khomeini. We need to examine briefly the reaction of some of these and other stateless Muslim communities and, in doing so, comment on some of the underlying political trends in the Muslim world. We shall return to Khomeini's stance in the penultimate section before concluding with an assessment of the British Muslim position.

Let us begin with the Saudis. It was in early October 1988 that Faiyazuddin Ahmad of the Leicester-based Islamic Foundation, after receiving information from a friend in India, flew to Saudi Arabia to instigate a Saudi reaction against *The Satanic Verses*. In the weeks that followed Saudi Arabia, like Pakistan, Egypt, Somalia, Sudan, Malaysia, Qatar, Indonesia and South Africa, banned both the book and entry by its author.

Throughout October the pro-Saudi lobby in the United Kingdom met regularly to condemn the deeply anti-Islamic sentiment expressed in *The Satanic Verses*. In London, Dr Syed Pasha, secretary of the Union of Muslim Organisations, called a crisis meeting and launched a national campaign. In a letter to the Prime Minister he called for prosecution of the author and the publishers. In early November Mrs Thatcher replied that there were no grounds for prosecution under existing British law.

Towards the end of November 1988 ambassadors in

London from several Arab Muslim countries met to formulate a comprehensive anti-Rushdie strategy. They were briefed by the Saudi diplomat Sheikh Mughram al-Ghamdi, Director of the Islamic Cultural Centre based at the Regent's Park Mosque in London. The ambassadors, all trustees of the Islamic Cultural Centre, agreed to campaign peacefully and called, rather weakly, for a state ban. In the weeks that followed, there were meetings with MPs and British government officials. By late December the ambassadors of Pakistan, Qatar and Somalia, along with the Saudi Director of the Regent's Park Mosque, had already formally protested to the Home Office.

Just before the end of 1988 Sir Patrick Mayhew, the Attorney-General, told the Muslims, through Dr Pasha, that the publication of *The Satanic Verses* constituted no criminal offence. In early January 1989 Lord Mackay, the Lord Chancellor, informed the Muslim campaigners that blasphemy, being a criminal offence, came under Home Office responsibility. On 1 February 1989 Douglas Hurd unequivocally stated that the blasphemy law would not be extended to cover non-Anglican sanctities. The Saudi lobby, like other Muslims in Britain, had knocked on every official door.

Khomeini's intervention in mid-February raised the issue to a new level of seriousness both for the West and for the Saudis. The Ayatollah had condemned the book, the author and its publishers. What had the Saudis done? Muslims openly began to question whether the ruling Saudi dynasty was worthy to be called guardians of the two holy cities. Towards the end of February letters even from non-Muslims, condemning *The Satanic Verses*, began to appear in the British media. At about the same time the Saudi organisation Rabita al-Alam al-Islami finally declared that Rushdie's book contained 'affronts and assaults on the Islamic creed' and 'infringed the sanctities of the Islamic faith . . . punishable in any country ruled by a system, constitution and laws that protect people's rights and dignity'.

Meanwhile, in Saudi Arabia itself, a leading court scholar, Sheikh Abdul Aziz bin Abdullah bin Baz, urged that Rushdie be tried *in absentia*, under Islamic law in a Muslim country, on charges of 'heretical crimes against the House of Islam'. Lesser Arab religionists began to demand, unrealistically, Rushdie's extradition, while their governments had imposed a ban on his entry. Khomeini was no longer the only Islamic jurist to have condemned *The Satanic Verses* and its author.

After an intensified and unified world-wide campaign against Rushdie's book, the Jeddah-based Organisation of the Islamic Conference (OIC) reluctantly agreed to put the issue on its agenda. The OIC, established in 1969, is essentially a club of pro-Western Islamic countries. Few of its recommendations ever affect international events or policies. However, for what it is worth, the OIC passed a resolution on 16 March to defuse the universal outrage felt by Muslims over the Rushdie affair. In it, the 45 member states condemned *The Satanic Verses* and its author and called for concerted action to combat blasphemy against Islam and the prostitution of the reputation of Islamic personalities. The leaders of the member states were exhorted to ban the book, and boycott all Penguin publications unless the offending book was immediately withdrawn. The declaration was not mandatory and, in real terms, had little effect. Indeed, some non-Islamic countries like India and South Africa had taken stronger measures.

When I wrote 'An Open Letter Concerning Blasphemy' immediately after the publication of *The Satanic Verses*, I predicted that Arab religious personnel, particularly the Saudi guardians of Islam's holy sites, would strongly condemn Rushdie and his publishers. Khomeini seemed too preoccupied with the rebuilding of post-revolutionary Iran to bother with monitoring the Rushdie episode. In the event, I was completely mistaken. But I was in good company. For the entire Muslim population of the world was amazed by the silence of the Arab governments and associated religionists at a time when a writer, protected by the West, had opened up the heart of Muslim conviction for universal ridicule. That King Fahd and the Kuwaitis should welcome Prince Charles and Lady Diana during their Saudi and Gulf tour and assure them of unconditional Saudi and Arab friendship with Britain was interpreted by many Muslims to be a peculiarly treacherous act. Many Muslim commentators reminded us of the Saudis' keen displeasure at the showing of the film *Death of a Princess* on British television. The film was, wrongly no doubt, interpreted to be an insult to the Saudi royal family; the Saudis immediately withdrew their ambassador, threatened to break diplomatic relations and indeed even hinted they might impose economic sanctions. The film was, accordingly, withdrawn by the British authorities.

In the Rushdie affair, the Saudis adopted an unduly soft approach, failing even to protest strongly to the British government. Many Muslims accused the Saudis, who belong to the Wahhabi sect of Islam, as having, like all Wahhabis, no adequate appreciation of the greatness of Muhammad. Religious sectarianism apart, it is hard to resist the conclusion that the reputation of their family is, for the Saudis, more worthy of protection than the reputation of the Prophet Muhammad. The fact is doubly surprising when we note that Muhammad is not only a supreme figure of Islamic history but also, in the case of the Saudis, a national hero who brought their nation to permanent prominence in one of the major conquests of history.

The Saudi, and more generally Arab, response has been conspicuously slow, gentle and undemonstrative. Even the OIC resolution was passed in the wake of a massive and concerted world-wide campaign by the ordinary powerless Muslim masses. And it is not unfair to speculate that the OIC's member states were, like their Western allies, concerned solely with the risks to their vital political, economic and strategic interests. It is noteworthy that while all Islamic states have banned *The Satanic Verses*, few leaders have condemned it or its author. The state ban is often imposed simply in order to appease the anger of the ruled Muslim masses. Indeed, the Saudi ban on *The Satanic Verses* is, in real terms, hollow. For the Saudis routinely ban books; even imports of sacred literature (like the Koran) are prohibited if printed outside the Saudi Kingdom.

Iranian commentators have been particularly loud and unequivocal in their condemnation of the silence of the Saudis. On 29 March two Muslims in Belgium—an Imam and his assistant—were killed for opposing Khomeini's *fatwa*. It is widely (and plausibly) believed that Iranians were responsible for the assassinations. Tensions between pro-Iranian and pro-Saudi Muslim organisations have increased world-wide, including those in Europe and the Far East.

The fact is, of course, that any agitation on a large scale could, if unchecked, lead to a serious sense of grievance and eventually pose a threat to the political stability of several Arab régimes. Iranian commentators have repeatedly warned that any politicisation of the Muslim peoples will, in effect, encourage in the long-term a radicalisation that may well inspire Khomeini-style revolutions. The threat of Islamic fundamentalism to some Arab governments, such as Egypt, Kuwait and Saudi Arabia, is indeed all too real. It is a clear comment on the popularity and power of militant Islam that, notwithstanding Western pressures to condemn Khomeini, few Muslim leaders or religionists have issued a verdict against Khomeini's judgement.

7

We need to examine briefly the reaction of several nations with large Muslim populations, and, in doing so, identify the competing internal forces of Islamic militancy as well as militant secularity in the Muslim world.

It is a sign of the times that a project for rewriting Arab history, without any reference to Islam, was being launched in the Iraqi city of Baghdad early in 1989. Meeting under the chairmanship of Dr Mustafa al-Najar, the executive council of the Bureau for Writing Arab History decided that Arabs constitute a distinct racial group whose present and past achievements needed fuller appreciation. Distortions allegedly introduced by Iranian and Western orientalist scholars were to be excised; all authentic writing must refer exclusively to Arab sources. Revealingly, throughout the Council's deliberations, Islam is never mentioned in any context—as if it were not Islam that brought the Arabs to prominence for the first (and indeed only) time in their history.

Apart from Iran and the Lebanon, the only other citadel

of Islamic fundamentalism is of course Egypt. The Rushdie affair comes at a time of increased tensions between Egyptian 'moderates' and their Muslim fundamentalist opponents. Although Islam is the official religion of Egypt with the Islamic law (Shari'ah) the main source of Egyptian legislation (Article 2, The Constitution), Islam has in practice virtually no influence on government policy. The fundamentalist Muslims have therefore declared that Egyptian society is infidel (*takfir*). Significantly, three prominent Muslim scholars at the al-Azhar Islamic seminary in Cairo issued a *fatwa* declaring that the charge of infidelity was invalid when issued against a whole society as opposed to an individual or group of individuals.

In mid-March, Dr Sayed Tantawi, the Mufti of Cairo and Imam at the al-Azhar seminary issued his *fatwa* concerning Salman Rushdie. He opted for what the West calls a moderate stance, condemning the book's contents in fairly mild terms while virtually exonerating Rushdie. One could have safely expected such a soft verdict from the Egyptian government's supreme authority on Islamic law. The reaction of the official government-employed Muslim clergy to the Rushdie provocation has been the straw that broke the camel's back for the radical Islamic groups in Egypt. There have been passionate calls for a *jehad* on a corrupt political order.

In Egypt there are only two kinds of Muslims: those who support the government's policies and those who are in jail. And the fundamentalists are mostly in jail. Only the 'moderates' are free to practise Islam. For their Islam poses no threat to vested Western interests. The 'moderate' Islamic elements in the Middle East are, in official Egyptian as well as Western interpretations, the ones considered harmless to the West.

In Algeria too, Islamic fundamentalism is seen as a major threat to the stability of the state. In recent months, the Algerian authorities have been engaged in several attempts to weaken the forces likely to inspire an Islamic resurgence. In fact, the recent constitutional reforms approved at a national referendum in Algiers are primarily designed to isolate Islamic groups from the left-wing labour groups.

Since the country's independence from France in 1962, the

Islamic factions have often joined forces, for purely pragmatic reasons, with the left-wing groups lobbying for justice and reform. (The pragmatic decision to unite Muslims and Marxists was also an ingredient in Khomeini's revolutionary overthrow of the Shah in Iran.) Islamic and left-wing activists jointly organised the unofficial strikes and riots in October 1987 that challenged Colonel Chadli Benjedid's régime. The government knows that behind the October unrest, in which 500 people died, was a powerful coalition of radical Muslim and militant labour groups.

Article 40 of the new constitution forbids the formation of political associations directed against state interests. Accordingly socialism is abolished as the state ideology; but the new constitution confers upon trade unions in the public sector the right to strike. This measure seems to be part of an attempt to satisfy left-wing demands and thereby isolate the specifically Muslim forces of protest. A major concern of the Algerian rulers, along with their Arab and Western allies, is to preserve the essentially secular nature of the political institutions. And Islamic fundamentalism poses a serious threat to that aspiration since the Islamic groups want to have a constitution based on Islamic law (shari'ah).

The Turkish reaction to the Rushdie affair can only be properly assessed against the background of a recent attempt by the masses to reassert their Islamic identity. The imposed secularism of Kemal Ataturk and his followers has long been resented by the ordinary Turks who, by and large, remain loyal to Islam. In March 1989, at the height of the Rushdie affair, there were several demonstrations in Ankara against a supreme court's decision to revoke the law permitting women to wear the veil on university campuses. Turkey's President Kenan Evren, who sees Islamic radicalism as a great threat to national security, had insisted on the abrogation of the law permitting female students to wear a headscarf. At the demonstration, male and female marchers called for Evren's resignation and shouted, 'Evren and Rushdie go hand in hand'.

In Bursa, the Ottoman Empire's first capital, there were many displays of popular anger over *The Satanic Verses*. The

Turkish authorities' decision to permit the screening of *The Last Temptation of Christ* as part of the eighth annual film festival was seen as a further provocation. Muslim critics in Turkey have long been protesting about the sexual permissiveness that secularity has brought—with Turkey being the only Muslim country openly importing pornographic materials and even printing a Turkish edition of *Playboy*. The Rushdie affair comes at a time of increased official hostility to traditional Islam as Kemalist secularist forces retreat in the face of a new assertion of Islamic values by ordinary Turks. The Turkish government's recent decision to welcome Muslims of Turkish descent expelled from Bulgaria had been its only redeeming action in the eyes of its Muslim fundamentalist opponents until the authorities eventually capitulated and banned *The Satanic Verses*.

In Pakistan there have been several violent protest rallies over Rushdie's book. The Islamabad riots on 12 February, in which six people were killed, may well have prompted Khomeini to issue his *fatwa*. The Islamabad riots were followed by riots in Lahore, Peshawar and Karachi. In early March popular anger against Rushdie was caught up in ethnic animosity between various factions, especially in Karachi. A bomb went off at the British Council Library in Peshawar in mid-March.

Pakistan's Prime Minister Benazir Bhutto was in China at the time of the February protests held in front of the American Cultural Centre in Islamabad. She interpreted the anti-Rushdie protests as being a part of the right-wing Islamic lobby's attempt to destabilise her government. After the mysterious death of General Zia-ul-Haq, the pro-Saudi Islamic parties were defeated by Miss Bhutto's Pakistan People's Party in the November 1988 elections. It is probable that the right-wing politicians mounted the demonstrations to embarrass the pro-American factions in Bhutto's party. It is harder to believe that those who died in the demonstrations did so for purely political motives. At any rate, Miss Bhutto banned *The Satanic Verses* without condemning its author. Indeed, in a BBC radio interview, she accused opponents of Rushdie of being guilty of blasphemy! Unsurprisingly, Britain's

Foreign Secretary, Geoffrey Howe, voiced his approval of Miss Bhutto's stance on the Rushdie affair and, more generally, welcomed the full 'restoration of democracy' by Pakistan's allegedly new 'civilian' government.

In neighbouring India, *The Satanic Verses* was banned as early as October 1988. The secularist Muslim politician Syed Shahabuddin, a member of the opposition Janata Party, alerted the Indian government to Rushdie's book; Rajiv Gandhi reacted immediately. Apart from the fact that Gandhi was facing a general election—there are 150 million Muslims in India—he no doubt remembered how his mother had successfully brought libel charges against Rushdie's earlier prizewinning novel *Midnight's Children*. At any rate, India was among the first countries to ban the sale and distribution of the book. While it is an avowedly secular nation, Indian politicians wisely prohibited publication in order to avoid inter-religious strife.

8

Rushdie's loss of faith is not an unusual phenomenon. Countless Muslims have, under the impact of Western thought, repudiated Islamic ideals. The view that Muslim societies are inferior and irrational relics from a bygone age is by no means restricted to Western critics. The intellectual and political élite in Islamic lands—as in the Third World more generally— share the conviction that Islam patronises an outdated system of belief and practice. Most of the nationalist leaders who aspired for independence from European colonial rulers were themselves secular in outlook. After independence the Muslim world was placed in the custody of a secularised élite leadership sympathetic to the West's political goals.

The ruling élites in most Islamic countries flirt with the ideals and traditions of their former colonial masters. There is therefore a virtually complete rift between an educated leadership, entertaining a Eurocentric world-view, and the illiterate ruled classes, often passionately attached to traditional Islam. Even countries created specifically to be Islamic states, such as Pakistan and Algeria, have subsequently been ruled by a Westernised élite sympathetic to Western capitalism and secularity, and completely opposed to the ideals of the Muslim people they rule.

Many anti-Islamic politicians in the Muslim world none the less enjoy great popularity among the believing masses, because they carefully conceal their loss of faith. There are therefore countless Rushdies in the House of Islam. The Shah of Iran and his supporters were, to a man, atheists blindly imitating Western patterns of conduct. It is not in vain that Henry Kissinger once referred to the Shah as America's 'unconditional' ally. Indeed, the rulers of almost all contemporary Muslim nation-states are secularists committed to upholding Western interests.

With few exceptions, the nation-states labelled 'Islamic' are in reality neo-colonial sovereignties in which Muslim ambitions are severely mutilated. It is noteworthy that the freest Muslims live in the West and in Iran. Everywhere else, Islam is an outlawed political force. It is no exaggeration to call the Arab states proxies of the United States and Britain. Indeed one might even say that the leaders of many so-called Muslim countries are fellow conspirators with the West in their opposition to Islamic forces in their territories. Western critics must not allow their hatred of Khomeini to obscure a recognition of the truth about the realities of power in the Muslim world.

The reaction of Western governments to the Rushdie affair is understandable. For these governments' defence of Rushdie is itself part of their continuing defence of countless Rushdies all over the Muslim world. In all the client-states, Rushdies abound. And they need to be protected from the wrath of the Muslim masses. Once the peoples of Islam learn the truth about their rulers, Khomeini-style revolutions need not remain confined to Iran or the Lebanon.

It is no coincidence that the most extreme *fatwa* comes from Khomeini. A unique feature of contemporary Iranian society is its radical reversal of the roles of secularity and religion. In the essentially secular order established by the colonial masters of the Muslim world, Islam was to be allowed to survive, even thrive, as a sub-culture. Khomeini's revolution re-establishes the supremacy of Islamic culture while relegating Western culture to the status of a tolerated aberration. For in major Iranian cities, Western cultural tendencies still co-exist with Islamic ones. This is in sharp contrast to other so-called Islamic states—notably Egypt, Pakistan and Saudi Arabia—where Islam is reduced to an item of piety in the private sector. Khomeini's Iran is the only country where the Christianising of Islam, so to speak, has been decisively challenged.

The victory of Western colonialism over Islamic states is at root the victory of powerful secularised nations over weak secularised nations. The political potential of Islam has not been drastically reduced by the triumph of Western secularity. For virtually none of the so-called Islamic states, other than Iran, allows Islam a say in its political policies. The Iranian Revolution, even gone wrong, proves that Islam can never be controlled by secular powers, for its religious enthusiasm can never be drastically reduced. It is Islam, as a unified enterprise of faith and power, that inspires the Afghans in their struggle against the Russian aggression; it is Islam that sustains the Palestinians' *Intifadah* when the secularised leadership has given in to Israel. A preacher such as Sheikh Abdul Karim Obeid is more dangerous than a 'terrorist' such as Yasser Arafat or a spectacularly wealthy ruler such as King Fahd. In the Middle East, rich men can be powerless while poor preachers can move mountains. And the Israelis know it.

Fundamentalist Islam as a unified enterprise of private faith and political allegiance deserves to be properly assessed. Western critics fail to appreciate the intellectual and moral credentials of fundamentalist Islamic positions because they short-circuit all critical thought as soon as the term appears. Take, for example, the portrait of Khomeini in the West. The Iranian revolutionary has been branded a complete devil in all the obituaries in the leading papers. Yet that extremism is no different from the extremism of Muslims who exaggerate the depravity and corruption of the West. Both assessments are wildly naïve, stereotyped, and indeed create more puzzles than they solve. The devotion to Khomeini televised in June

1989 at his funeral surely deserves to be placed in perspectives other than those of a cynicism that brands other folks' passion as mere fanaticism. Yet fanaticism too can be defensible — if it is about great ideals rather than mere trivialities.

Western appraisals of fundamentalist Islam betray bias and often complete ignorance even in their choice of political vocabulary. To argue that Khomeini issued a *fatwa* to dislodge the 'moderates' from any ascendancy within the Iranian political order is to misuse language — and to misunderstand the nature of Iranian society. There can be no question about Khomeini's sincerity in delivering his verdict — though even great jurists can be mistaken. As for the so-called moderates he is supposed to be challenging, one needs to know what is meant by moderation. Moderation is a virtue in Islamic ethics. It implies balance and fairness in judgement; it is not equivalent to opportunism or laxity in conduct. To Western commentators, all individuals harmless to the West, no matter how extremist in other ways, are moderates. The risk and indeed absurdity in such use of language is obvious. Thus, for example, Iran's Hashemi Rafsanjani was classed as a moderate by the West. Suddenly he ordered the killing of any five Americans or Europeans for every Palestinian killed by the Israelis; he was referred to more ambiguously after that as a 'moderate in Iranian terms'. The fact is of course that, for a Westerner, to call such a man moderate in any terms is to misuse language or, perhaps, to indulge a private sense of humour.

Khomeini has been a favourite target of Western resentment for over a decade. Yet few Western biographies of the late Iranian revolutionary do him justice. During the Rushdie affair there were scores of articles about the man and his faith. After all, Khomeini *was* fascinating: a man in his seventies leading an Islamic revolution, after years of exile, equipped only with the famous nail-clipper — and the will to martyrdom. Yet no biographer could develop the imaginative sympathy with his ideals necessary for any objective assessment of his achievement.

An alternative account is badly needed. On every score, whether one welcomes it or rejects it, the achievements of Khomeini's Islamic militancy are colossal. He is the only

Be Careful with Muhammad!

man—a poet, theologian and jurist in one—to have built a theocracy since the Renaissance. To question the political legitimacy of all contemporary political patterns—whether dynastic, dictatorial or democratic—in the name of religious principles requires not only a great political will but also an exceptional degree of mental independence. The West is alarmed by the militancy and 'terrorism' of leaders like Khomeini and Ghadaffi; and quite rightly so. But this militancy is primarily mental, not merely military. Khomeini was mentally free enough to refuse to interpret the whole world from a Eurocentric perspective that, rightly or wrongly, sets the mental fashion of virtually all of the world's contemporary ruling élite. For all his other errors, the Ayatollah did not make the mistake of sending his sons and grandsons to Oxford, Cambridge or Harvard.

Khomeini's Iran may well be seen as a medieval theocracy by Western observers. Yet one needs to rise above one's ethnocentrism to see what cultural memories theocracy evokes in the Muslim mind. For theocracy is as precious to Muslims as democracy is to Westerners. The West rightly remembers theocracy with a collective shudder. Muslims may well have the right, for reasons historical as well as contemporaneous, to react differently. Certainly the view that only secular postures of power lead to humility in matters of statecraft is questionable in an age that has witnessed the arrogant brutality of two major wars, Hiroshima, and the increasingly darkening shadow of nuclear holocaust. Virtually all the major tragedies of the twentieth century—possibly our worst century so far—have been caused by secular and nationalist ambitions. Even the much lamented Iran-Iraq war was not a purely religious struggle. There is much to be said, in retrospect, for the view that the socialist nation-state of Iraq, as a vassal of the capitalist West, was the aggressor.

Westerners must be careful with men like Khomeini—but for the right reasons. There is on the ideological level a tremendous psychic tension between the West and fundamentalist Islam. A certain kind of power complex in the Western mind leads to a radical repudiation of Khomeini and all his works. Who was Khomeini to stand up to the West and say

92

whatever he thought was right? In an age of neo-colonial domination of the Muslim world by puppet régimes owing allegiance to Western powers, it is impossible to avoid some admiration for Khomeini.

In the final analysis the issue is to do with two world-views, both aristocratic in outlook, both bent on imperialism and proselytisation. Khomeini was no less passionate about empire-building than the Americans he denounced. Western commentators naturally prefer their own brand of imperialism to that of their opponents, but the instinct for domination is not foreign to either party. 'One goes "west"', writes Fazlun Khalid in a brilliant piece, 'wherever one goes'. Those who reject or resist the mental imperialism of the West are dubbed fundamentalists. Khomeini was certainly a fundamentalist. For he wanted us to go East—wherever we go.

9

Should Muslims in the West endorse Khomeini's *fatwa*? It is noteworthy that the Iranian verdict does not demand the banning of *The Satanic Verses*. Khomeini concentrates on the person of the author (and his publishers) rather than on the offensive publication itself. British and American Muslims, by contrast, have concentrated on the book rather than its author. Rushdie doesn't matter—to put the point rather arrogantly. For Muslims in the West, the state banning or voluntary withdrawal of *The Satanic Verses* would be a satisfactory resolution. This is why Rushdie's apology offered immediately after the issuing of the *fatwa* has not been accepted: as long as the book remains in print and on sale Muslims will continue to protest.

If Rushdie could be tried in a court of law, whether in the West or in an Islamic land, then that would be considered a bonus. But the primary aim is to have his book withdrawn. Thus, for example, an influential Muslim community in New Zealand has successfully campaigned for a ban on the import of *The Satanic Verses*; accordingly, Muslims in New Zealand have dropped their enmity towards Rushdie himself. Unfortunately no other Western country has yet followed suit. Some

Western commentators have argued that the repeal of Khomeini's *fatwa* is a condition of negotiations with the Muslims. Yet it seems unfair to ask British Muslims to reject what they have never endorsed. It is true that a number of individuals, in a moment of anger, endorsed Khomeini's *fatwa*. But 'death to Rushdie' has never been the official position of any British Muslim authority or organisation. To be sure, individual Muslims may well wish to disown as immoral the threat to Rushdie's life. But that is a matter of private judgement. Muslims in the West cannot influence the decisions of the Iranian government.

The most difficult thing in the Rushdie affair is to maintain a consistent and convincing moral position. In Granada Television's *Hypotheticals* (screened on 30 May 1989) it became rapidly clear that many of those involved in the affair entertained a confused moral stance. Thus, for example, the Muslim participants, Dr Kalim Saddiqui and Yusuf Islam, seemed ambivalent in their response to questions about Khomeini's *fatwa*. Granted that they endorsed it as theologically valid, would they implement it in a country outside the House of Islam? Were they not under an obligation to attach priority to British law? Both tended to give or imply evasive responses that betrayed a lack of clarity in their ethical outlook.

In one sense, the reaction of the British government to Khomeini's death threat was entirely wrong and distracting. For the fact that outside powers (such as Iran) were interfering should also have been the occasion for recognising the gravity of the situation, of the profundity of Muslim indignation at home. Britain has a sizeable Muslim population which claims citizenship. Since they were the first, naturally, to agitate against *The Satanic Verses*, shouldn't the government do something to satisfy their demands? The death threat and the hysterical Western reaction to it together served to marginalise the real debate—namely the state banning or voluntary withdrawal of a book calculated to demean members of a distinct group in their own (and others') eyes. Where there's a will, there's a way, indeed a thousand ways; if not, a thousand excuses.

5   What's Wrong with Fundamentalism?

1

It didn't take Rushdie to teach Westerners that fundamentalism is a dirty word. There are countless commentators who have for a decade or so condemned fundamentalist options in all the three theisms of Judaism, Christianity, and Islam. But it is Islamic fundamentalism that remains the favourite target of Western resentment. For fundamentalist Islam increasingly makes the headlines: a sentence of execution is passed on a foreign novelist; leaders of Islamic countries, seen as client-states of the West, are assassinated by members of radical Muslim groups; Europeans travelling in the Lebanon are accused of spying and are kidnapped; American airliners are hijacked, and so on.

Although many writers would condemn fundamentalist versions of all faiths, it is undeniable that Islamic fundamentalism is almost always judged with prejudicial rigour. Take, for example, V. S. Naipaul's *A Turn in the South* (published by Viking in 1989) in which he explores Christian fundamentalism in the United States. Naipaul is very generous to born-again Christian fundamentalists who are described as good and sincere. This is in sharp contrast to his earlier propagandist travelogue, *Among the Believers: An Islamic Journey*, dealing with Muslim fundamentalism in several Islamic lands. *Among the Believers* is saturated with the predictable prejudices of a Westernised Hindu. Yet the book has been wrapped in praise by Western reviewers. Relying entirely on anecdotal evidence, Naipaul sees Muslim fundmentalists as foolish and insincere, taking false comfort in the oversimplifications of an outdated faith, hoping to reap the benefits of modernity without paying the usual price.

Western students of Islam need to be very careful in their assessments of Islam. A propagandist political vocabulary, so routinely employed in discussions of Islam, needs to be challenged in the interests of objectivity. Islam is not just a catalogue of rigid rules about alcohol, theft and sexuality. It is a way of life, a unified enterprise of faith and power—with deep religious resources for sustaining a variety of moods of authentic piety.

Both in popular and academic writing in the West, there has long been an unargued assumption that fundamentalist interpretations of Islam can have no adequate intellectual credentials. Both secularised Christian and liberal critics of Islam have concurred that fundamentalist Islam patronises morally indefensible attitudes. Unfortunately, in Western universities, the protagonists in debates about Islamic fundamentalism are, without exception, Jewish and Christian theists, simplistic Muslims ignorant of Western thought or Third World champagne socialists repudiating the faith of their forefathers. Authentic Muslims of intellectual ability are systematically excluded. It is high time we explored the virtues of fundamentalism.

2

'Is there anything about Islam you *don't* like?' A Christian colleague asked me this question in the sure expectation that the response of a passionate Muslim would be: 'No. I like all of it.' The correct answer, of course, is exactly the opposite. 'Yes. Lots of things. It's a tough religion.'

The point is significant. Islam does not claim to be a religion of comfort or convenience. One dislikes its obligations often enough. Some of its claims are, in worldly eyes, scandals. But that is Islam. There are within every vision certain beliefs that look to outsiders like prejudices. Yet, in the last analysis, one must defend these too.

At another level, one changes human nature to suit religious demand; one must not alter religious demand to suit our human, all too human, wishes. One of the cardinal defects of modern Protestant thought has been its failure to grasp this truth. To be fair, for most Muslims, Islam is a 'Friday religion'—they feel particularly pious on Friday afternoons but fail to sustain these feelings for the rest of the week. But Islam is none the less in much more evidence in the daily lives of those who call themselves Muslims than Christianity is in the daily lives of those who profess Christianity. And it is largely to do with a recognition of the principle that God's ordinances are to be fulfilled no matter how severe the temptations to lapse and fail.

I understand 'fundamentalism' to be the position that the scriptural canon contains a basic source of wholly correct guidance. Such a view may, to choose less loaded terminology, be labelled integralist. It may reasonably be maintained by a modernist as well as by a traditionalist or fundamentalist believer; the usual contrast between the two is wrongly drawn.

Fundamentalist handling of sacred literature is often derided, particularly by secularised Christian believers, as going down a religious cul-de-sac. 'The "light" in the Enlightenment was', as the Rt Rev. Lesslie Newbigin reminds us, 'real light'. The advance of rational thought and the spectacular increase in the scope and authority of the sciences of man and nature have together served to expose as embarrassingly fantastic—if not utterly false or incoherent—some of the non-religious trappings of the faith. We can, it is said, no longer accept in the light of recently acquired sophistication, the traditional notion of infallible dictation of scripture; the Bible has no intrinsic authority independent of the verdict of secular thought. Conservative confidence in the authenticity of the *religious* core of revelation, the contention concludes, can none the less remain intact since the false non-religious elements are to be simply identified and then expunged.

Unfortunately, however, distinctions between religious truth and secular error are rarely so neat and obliging as to coincide exactly with the wishes of contemporary Christian apology. If a book can be fallible in its claims about astronomy and biology, there is no reason why it should be infallible in its pronouncements on religious doctrine. In fact, of course, without begging the central question at stake, it is impossible to sift out the religious message which is presumed to be true from the culturally conditioned irrelevances presumed to be false. There may be motives for establishing a coincidence between the essence of a faith and just exactly those scandals to the intellect which today's worldly folk will tolerate. But there are no grounds for doing so.

For all Muslims, as for pre-Enlightenment Christians, faith should be an 'all or nothing affair'. The reasons are as decisive as they are simple. One cannot properly endorse the authoritative integrity of a partly fallible scripture. Muslims quite rightly interpret the Koran to be an error-free corpus undiluted by human factors external to its incidence. Fundamentalism, far from being a dead option, actually conceals the only defensible attitude towards what one takes to be the word of God.

This view of faith as an 'all or nothing affair' is very much open to misunderstanding. My defence of fundamentalism published in the *Observer* on Easter Sunday 1989 has been widely criticised, particularly by Christians. There were two major reservations which deserve a brief mention. Firstly, critics argued that it was not clear how one identifies the alleged fundamentals of Islam and whether or not these fundamentals, once identified, were properly subject to the kind of reform or development essential to reflective religion. Secondly, there were some Islamic doctrines, it was argued, that seemed to authorise intolerance towards members of other faiths and indeed towards women. Could such doctrines be defended?

The answer to the first question is simple. The Koran is the only fully authoritative source in Islam. A Muslim believer must accept it as a miracle of reason and speech and attempt to live by its rules. If a believer, male or female, finds some of its rules and claims unacceptable, he or she must still feel religiously obliged to contend with his or her doubts and weaknesses. The experience of such religious puzzles is a form of mental temptation that is a relatively normal trial in the life of faith. A believer is not permitted to take conscientious objection to what he or she sees as the word of God—for God is above human conscience. However, a believer may exercise his or her own judgement in assessing the moral worth of the Prophet's life and the received Islamic traditions of scholarship and piety. All sources, other than the scripture, are human and therefore fallible even though these may still be interpreted as having normative significance for the conduct of ordinary believers. An individual believer is also permitted to disagree with the consensus of his or her whole community provided that, according to certain agreed standards, he or she can claim to be learned in the scripture of Islam. Such individuals are usually exempt from obedience to the law (Shari'ah) but there is no reason to think that many of them exist in the modern world.

The issue of Muslim intolerance has recently been the subject of bitter commentary by Christians and liberals and of equally bitter rejoinder by Muslim apologists. Islam certainly has an ethic of co-existence with societies bearing revealed scriptures. The aim of Muslim imperialism has always been conquest rather than conversion. Thus, the Islamic record has been honourably distinguished, from its very inception, by its lenient ascendancy in dealings with vanquished Jewish and Christian communities. Even hostile critics concede that Muslims have been far more inclined, than their religious cousins, towards peace and reconciliation in the Holy Land. Beyond that, the failings of Muslims are merely a part of the failings of our common humanity.

Christians have, surprisingly, cast the first stone here. Yet the Christian record is, as many modern Christians themselves concede, utterly deplorable. For though the Christian community has rarely defended intolerance as an ideal, it would be difficult to find many among its members in the past who have avoided intolerance in practice. Christian tolerance may well be a virtue inspired by a love for justice and forbearance. Yet it is too often found only in lands and epochs where the faith is dead or dying. (Christians are not known for their lenience in Northern Ireland, South Africa and the Lebanon.) Could the real motives be indifference and apathy, themselves rooted in loss of faith? The tolerance of a faith should be manifest in its age of enthusiasm as well as at a time of decline.

The question of Muslim women's relation to their men, in equality or otherwise, has exercised many critics, both within and outside the Muslim world. It is widely believed that Islamic fundamentalism assigns second-class status to female populations. That Muslim women are in fact severely oppressed and often denied even basic human rights in Muslim countries such as India and Pakistan is so blatantly obvious as to make all apologetic denial totally unconvincing. The critique of fundamentalism, however, goes well beyond that in claiming that Islamic doctrine is designed to oppress women, no matter how charitably one interprets it.

This is a problematic charge. While one might reasonably claim that the Koran envisages a society under male leadership, it is not clear that its doctrines are necessarily incompatible with some forms of women's emancipation. Certainly, the sexual puritanism of many Muslim lands is entirely contrary to the spirit of the sacred volume.

The traditional Muslim custom of segregating female society from the male population—in order to protect women against aggressive kinds of male desire—has led to charges of sexual apartheid. But one must not judge too hastily here. For the aim of the veil is to create a truly erotic culture in which one dispenses with the need for the artificial excitement that pornography provides. Certainly, Islam condemns the commercial exploitation of women that reduces them to little more than a cause of male desire.

There are deep and controversial issues here. Muslim women themselves must now attempt to interpret the sacred text and question the traditional male bias that has patronised their oppression for so long. But it is well to remember that there will be scandals here; some divine imperatives may seem, to a modern secularised conscience, demanding and harsh. A few scandals remain for all believers—men and women alike.

3

Respect for other people of faith is an article of faith in Islam. It is, therefore, with justified resentment that Muslims have noted the lack of sympathy displayed by other religious groups, notably Christians, during the Rushdie provocation.

Why do Christians, as fellow religious believers, also abet and second abusive assaults on an established religious tradition?

Apart from a few French Roman Catholics such as the Archbishop of Lyons, few influential Christians have sympathised with the Muslims over *The Satanic Verses* affair. Though Muslims had been among the first to protest at the showing of Scorsese's controversial *The Last Temptation of Christ*, they received scant support from Christians in their own hour of trial. The established and legally protected Church of England has only mildly condemned Rushdie's attack on Islam while loudly condemning the Muslim style of protest.

In one sense, the Christian reaction is to be expected. There has been a titanic struggle between the two missionary faiths of Islam and Christianity for the last 1500 years; and my enemy's enemy is my friend. The ideological battle between the Crescent and the Cross is by no means over either in Africa and the Third World or in Europe and North America.

In other ways, the Christian reservation about the Islamic protest has been puzzling. The Christian establishment tried to censor D. H. Lawrence's novel *Lady Chatterley's Lover* and Thomas Hardy's *Jude the Obscure*. Their reasons were far less substantial: the former because of the use of four-letter words and the latter because it was seen, perhaps wrongly, as an implied attack on the sanctity of the institution of marriage. The Bishop of Wakefield burnt a copy of Hardy's novel. Nor is this a relic of some past age of Christian enthusiasm. Both attempts at censorship were made in the twentieth century. And as late as the 1970s, Christians successfully sued a publication for linking Christ with homosexuality.

Affronted Muslim believers were never more irritated than when Christian believers joined the Liberal Inquisition. Surely, the Christians as religious people would and should understand the anguish of their fellow theists. What was their excuse for persecuting the Muslims?

So loud and clear is the voice of mockery in *The Satanic Verses* that Muslims, including myself, remain amazed at Western, particularly Christian reaction. To be sure, several

Christians did recognise that Muslims did have a right to be severely offended. After all, there are limits to mockery. One might mock the Pope or doubt his infallibility: but it would be immoral to mock Christ. The Rt Rev. Lesslie Newbigin of Birmingham and the Rev. Kenneth Cragg from Oxford both expressed concern at the intolerant treatment of Muslims by the host society.

Notwithstanding these few isolated examples of sympathy and sincerity, most Christian commentators behaved arrogantly. At the height of the affair, I suffered a personal crisis of conscience: I could not take the critics seriously. Were they merely sincere but misguided? Or insincere and misguided?

Several Christian writers have condescendingly argued that all this fuss over an admittedly offensive book shows that Muslims lack the self-confidence of the Christian mind. After all, Christians bore with dignity the provocation of *The Last Temptation of Christ*. Surely the Christian faith has not been undermined.

The truth is of course too obviously the other way. While Christian apologists continue to make a virtue out of a weakness, the continuous blasphemies against their faith have almost totally undermined it. No religion or ideology devoid of an internal temper of militant but constructive wrath can safeguard and perpetuate its heritage. Belief-systems, like biological organisms, must be fortified against external attack if they are to survive in a world addicted to the logic of coercion. It is only a comforting myth that the sword of Christian love is sharper than the enemy's sword of steel. In a world where evil assumes militant forms, good can only survive if it is equally militant in its defence. Vulnerability is, Christian apology notwithstanding, never the best proof of strength.

The central Christian misunderstanding in this area has been that somehow the militant wrath of Muslims is due to fear and internal anxiety rather than to confidence and a commitment to faith. The issue is significant. Is the militant Islamic temper merely reactionary and defensive? Or is it indeed the hallmark of the truly religious imagination?

The Satanic Verses does not threaten Islam. The cry of

Muslims springs from passion and wholesome enthusiasm rather than insecurity and dogmatism. To react against wanton ideological attack is a healthy sign indicating that the ideology is alive and well, that those who espouse it take it seriously. The lesson for the Christian conscience could hardly be clearer.

Nor will it do to say that God does not need human defence. It is true of course that God is above human insult in one sense; but there is another equally valid sense in which the believer is morally obliged to vindicate the reputation of God and his spokesmen against the militant calumnies of evil. Only then can he or she truly confess the faith. For faith is as faith does. In this matter, the Koran is bound to have the last word: God does not guide a people who sell his signs for a paltry price. Small wonder then that the Christian clergy are failing to preserve and transmit the faithful heritage.

4

Beneath a picture of the kidnapped Anglican Terry Waite, the caption reads: 'This man can't go to church this Sunday. What's your excuse?' The question, part of the Church of England's advertising campaign against religious indifference, is addressed to the Christian conscience but might we not borrow it to query the modern religious inclination in general? For in this age of widespread secularity and indifference to religious faith, there is no shortage of excuses. Yet the message of fundamentalist Islam still manages to bring the Friday traffic to a halt outside Cairo's overflowing mosques.

It is possible to state the vigour and enthusiasm of Islam as a fact—rather than as a boast. Muslim religionists are often derided as ignorant and obscurantist. But they have successfully protected orthodoxy against the forces of compromise and dilution. The heritage of Islam has been successfully transmitted to its modern custodians. It is now a powerful force within the world, inspiring martyrdom at the highest rate of any living faith.

One might lament the lack of thinkers in contemporary fundamentalist Islam. Islamic doctrine, wisely, discourages inappropriate kinds of curiosity; and orthodoxy encourages 'safe' thoughts. Muslims generally refuse to countenance any subtlety of mind or will that might undermine Islam. There is, if you like, a kind of deliberately cultivated self-protective naïveté which safeguards the faith in an age of mental adventurism. But, in any case, one must not exaggerate the importance of intellectuals for a religious tradition. A faith can survive indefinitely without thinkers—but not without martyrs. And there is no shortage of martyrs in Islam even in an allegedly godless twentieth century.

The liberal atheistic assumption that religion is on its deathbed has been decisively refuted by several events in the current century—including the Iranian Revolution and the Rushdie affair. Islam will continue to plague the labours of the liberals who are trying to replace God by enlightened man as the sole arbiter of moral norm.

The aim of the Liberal Inquisition has been to intimidate Muslims: all absolutist supernatural claims must yield to the alleged moral relativism of the liberal West. In fact, of course, one is merely replacing one absolutism with another, for liberalism is no less an absolute position than Islam. As we saw in Chapter 3, the liberal establishment is trying to capture the high moral ground by perpetuating the myth of its own superiority to all religion, particularly to Islam. Yet the irony of course is that the notion that self-styled and self-appointed liberal arbiters of what is the norm are the sole custodians of civilised values is itself illiberal. The Rushdie affair has, as an unintended consequence, confirmed that fact beyond a shadow of a doubt.

Contemporary secular man has emerged triumphant over all religious traditions—except Islam. Muslims refuse to accept the intellectual or cultural supremacy of the secular outlook. Hence, of course, the well-known hostility to practising Muslims. I know from my own experience in several Western countries that a 'moderate' Muslim is defined as one who does not take his faith seriously. Anyone who does is, on account of that fact alone, classed as a fanatic.

In the West, most Jews and Christians are not truly religious in outlook. They may fairly be described as secularised and humane capitalists who accept the political hegemony of the current system. Muslims are truly religious in outlook for they refuse to allow their faith to be relegated to the status of a tolerated sub-culture. Instead they still propose, no matter how unrealistically, manifestos for the Kingdom of God on earth—even in this age of secularity. It is undeniable that Christianity no longer controls the subversive movements of thought or action within the culture it has historically inspired. It has, in effect, been reduced to a sub-culture manipulated regularly by a secular nation-state.

If a dying Western Christianity accommodates secularism, a resurgent fundamentalist Islam challenges it. The Muslim response to Rushdie has successfully challenged the cultural and mental imperialism of the occidental mind. This alone can explain the sheer depth of liberal resentment against Muslims.

The West does not necessarily oppose Islamic fundamentalism in all political contexts. Thus, for example, the Americans have, for strategic reasons, supported the Afghan fundamentalists in their struggle against Russian expansionism. But, fundamentalism in Iran and the Lebanon is fiercely rejected by the West. Thus far, the Western acceptance of Islamic fundamentalism has depended on the political complexion of its associated movement. But, after the Rushdie affair, I would think that Islamic fundamentalism will be opposed in any and every form, no matter what its larger political alignment. It is too dangerous a force, for it has encouraged militancy among *all* believers, including Jews and Christians. After the Rushdie affair, many Christians recognise the need' for a militant post-Enlightenment church—and militant in the Islamic style. Many secretly recognise that to tolerate gratuitous abuse is indeed a matter for shame, not for pride.

Dangerous or not, Islamic fundamentalism is here to stay. It is wrong to assume that it is an isolated accident or an aberration of Muslim history. It is integral to Islam because only an integralist interpretation of Islam is convincing. Power and the political dimension are vital to Islam because, as a

faith, it has always resisted attempts to shelve it in the private
sector of purely personal devotion. The Kingdom of God is
not merely within you—it must be brought forth into the
human world.

6   Faith and Power

1

A Christian friend recently complained to me: 'I do wish Muslims would learn to develop a theology of powerlessness. We did—a long time ago. With God, nothing succeeds—like failure.'

With God, perhaps; but in the human context, as my Christian friend knew very well, the slogan is entirely different. Islam, like any other ideology, including Christianity, instinctively seeks (and occasionally enjoys) the sanction of political power. Unfortunately, in the West, Muslims constitute a powerless minority with severely restricted access to resources and opportunities in the world of employment, politics, learning and commerce. In Britain few Muslims exercise influence; almost none holds a position of power. Only a handful of them hold important posts in industry, the financial world, the universities, and the mass media. None has a say in Parliament. Unlike the traditionally established faith of Anglican Christianity, Islamic principles and values have always been systematically excluded from exercising any influence on the policies of the British government.

To be sure, there are individuals with Muslim-sounding names who hold a few positions of influence in contemporary Britain. But these men and women are militantly anti-Islamic, often consciously repudiating the faith of their forefathers. In most cases they are appointed more on grounds of ideological suitability than mere ability or expertise. It seems hardly unfair to accuse them of being, in effect, fellow conspirators working to undermine Islam and Muslim interests.

That there is a concerted attempt, throughout the Western world, to exclude able practising Muslims from positions of power and prestige cannot reasonably be denied. That Muslims are routinely subjected to unlawful discrimination on

107

grounds of religious affiliation is also a fact wholly beyond reasonable dispute. But Muslims, face to face with such injustice, do not cultivate a tragic impulse or the retiring mood. Islam encourages its votaries to strive for a just and prosperous social order here on earth. This religious motivation alone can explain the conspicuous moral purity of the anti-Rushdie campaign in the West. In thus seeking justice and equality of treatment, Muslims are close to the logic of the Prophet's own political activism. A Muhammad face to face with Pilate would have given the Roman chap a lot more to do than merely wash his hands.

2

One of the most remarkable features of the Rushdie affair has been its ordinariness. It did not begin as a scandal in high society only to be filtered down later to the masses. Rather, it began as an ordinary event with ordinary Muslims reacting to it. Indeed, in important ways, the issue has remained ordinary to the very end since the rich and potentially powerful Muslim groups and leaders in the Arab heartland of Islam have continued to maintain a puzzling silence. In some moods, one might forgive the British government for thinking that the only outrage is felt by a bunch of illiterate peasants in a remote northern city of England.

The Rushdie affair is at root a British affair, whatever its international ramifications. British Muslims have quite rightly resolved to lobby local MPs and Councillors in order to articulate their demands as citizens of a mature democracy. They have made their demands not as Muslims but primarily as British citizens; they have condemned governmental indifference in the name of social justice, not of religious imperative.

There is a sizeable Muslim constituency in modern Britain. There are just over a million Muslims here, most of whom are settled in the metropolitan areas of Yorkshire, the West Midlands and London. Over half of all British Muslims have originated in the Indian sub-continent, with roughly 70,000 settled in Bradford alone. Muslims actually constitute the largest 'immigrant' population in Britain today.

In the wake of the Rushdie affair, many Muslims have threatened to withdraw their electoral support from the Labour Party. Traditionally, of course, the majority of Muslims vote for Labour, though many Muslims uphold values more characteristic of the Conservatives. Though Muslims tend to emphasise the importance of commerce, encourage the promotion of community and family values, and endorse a conservative sexual ethic, they have, in the past at least, found the policies of the Labour Party more congenial to their overall interests. This is partly to do with the history of their settlement as immigrants from the Commonwealth. The majority of Muslims came from relatively poor and rural backgrounds in the Indian sub-continent in the 1960s and early 1970s to supply cheap labour for the British market. Some of them have begun to acquire wealth in the last decade. It is now rather problematic to categorise them as working-class since many of them do a manual job in Britain but run a small business here and own some property in the land of their origin. Their outlook is religiously as well as sexually conservative with a strong emphasis on scholarship and enterprise. This is hardly a description of a proletariat class in the sense in which most Western, particularly Marxist, commentators use the term.

It is likely that those Muslims who have acquired wealth or have entered the professions will vote for the Conservative Party. But, by and large, most will continue to opt for Labour. The majority are bound to remain poor since racist resentment results in the denial of many facilities and provisions to which Muslims are legally entitled as citizens of this Kingdom. Already poor, a significant number have dependents abroad who often look to them for regular financial support. The majority therefore remain underprivileged. To be fair, the British working-class is in as bad a shape financially, but it is at least spared the humiliation that racial discrimination brings in its train. Though the promise of class mobility remains for the poorer Muslims, in practice it is effectively empty, given the barriers erected by racist indignation at the new-found prosperity, real or imagined, of black immigrants from the Commonwealth.

The Rushdie affair may significantly transform Muslim political life in Britain. For if the affair has been responsible for arranging some unusual unions between the left and the right, it has also led to some equally unusual divorces. For one thing, Asian Muslims are no longer in the good books of the liberal anti-racists who once supported them in the name of equality and multi-culturalism. Many in the liberal left, who had encouraged local government to provide services to ethnic minorities including Muslims, now find themselves ranged on the opposite side, passionately defending Rushdie's right to 'freedom of speech'. Had Rushdie been white, the left would almost certainly have condemned his book as patronising prejudice against an already oppressed racial minority. But the colour of Rushdie's skin has completely clouded the liberal assessment of the affair. There may of course also be non-political, broadly personal, factors in the left's regard for Rushdie: he is not only the darling of the liberal press but also one of the most distinguished anti-racist campaigners; his videos and views are widely available and respected by practitioners in the race-relations industry. At any rate, the Muslim alignment with the left has always been viewed by both parties as a marriage of convenience; and so the divorce caused by the Rushdie saga has not led to accusations of betrayal or broken hearts.

The right has thoroughly enjoyed harassing Asians who are attacking a British author. The author's skin colour, which has long been an inconvenience for the establishment, is no longer a relevant consideration. The right is therefore in the odd position of having to defend a black man who is normally seen as an enemy. But my enemy's enemy is my friend.

In one sense, the distinctions within the political spectrum hardly matter. For neither the left nor the right has supported the Muslim campaign for the withdrawal of *The Satanic Verses*. In fact, it is not even possible to say which of the two major political parties has had greater sympathy. Understandably, British Muslim leadership has been frustrated when, in David Caute's characteristically perceptive words, 'wrestling with the baffling idioms and codes of the white chameleon, which is cunningly Christian yet secular, Conservative yet liberal, repressive yet permissive' (*New Statesman and Society*, 5 May, 1989).

British Muslims are a powerless minority. This is a bald assertion that no doubt needs qualification. For British Muslims are a powerless minority that forms a part of a potentially powerful global community, just as Catholics in Britain are a minority but retain links with a larger and more powerful universal fellowship. Even so, for most practical purposes, Muslims in Britain remain poor, isolated, and weak. In the Rushdie affair, their protest is a proof of their powerlessness; powerful groups do not need to demonstrate on the streets.

To be sure, Muslims are part of a larger British political constituency and, as citizens, wield some influence. In late March the Bradford Council of Mosques issued a communiqué: 'Support our anti-Rushdie campaign or lose votes.' The Paddock Ward by-election in Huddersfield was the first test of the new Muslim strategy. It failed to dislodge Labour from what was seen as a marginal seat. But the pressure from the Muslim electorate has not been entirely without effect; a number of MPs and Councillors in predominantly Muslim areas have endorsed some of the Muslim demands. Max Madden, Labour MP for Bradford West, has openly pleaded for the cancellation of the plans to bring out a paperback edition. Keith Vaz, Labour MP for Leicester East, has repeatedly called on Viking to withdraw *The Satanic Verses*. Vaz, a Catholic from India, has been vigorously attacked in left-wing circles and many have asked his constituency to elect another candidate at the next election who could better represent the 'official' Labour Party policy on race relations.

Muslim anger and frustration grew as government institutions reaffirmed their commitment to the continued publication of *The Satanic Verses* in a free and democratic Britain. Requests for legal enactment to protect Muslim sanctities were flatly rejected. Throughout March and April 1989, British Muslims became acutely aware of the extent of their political weakness. It became rapidly clear that no one listens to the powerless—unless they become a nuisance. And thus a very law-abiding Muslim community eventually decided to resort to a systematic political campaign involving, in the words of the pro-Iranian Muslim Institute's Director, Dr Kalim Saddique, 'symbolic breaking of the law and manipulation of the political process'. A concerned British Muslim leadership reminded Muslims of their obligations to obey the laws of their chosen country of citizenship; but they also reminded them of their duties as Muslims. The only feasible alternative was, therefore, a campaign of disobedience imitating other civil rights movements, in which existing unjust laws were broken as a prelude to reform and fairer legislation.

On 27 May 1989, roughly 30,000 Muslims converged on London's Parliament Square to demonstrate their justified resentment at the continued publication and sale of *The Satanic Verses* in Britain. There were minor incidents of violence and a few arrests. Several Western commentators dubbed the style of protest 'sub-continental'—a euphemism for violent and unruly. The newspapers carried more outbursts of white anger, from racists, liberals, and Conservatives alike. There were calls for a ban on demonstrations. Many white commentators, pretending to be offering analyses of the tension, were, in effect, beginning to issue threats to the Muslims. For example, Muslims were invited to step down their protests if they wanted to avoid a white backlash.

In mid-June, a protest rally in Bradford sparked off serious racial incidents in the city. There were renewed calls for increasing police powers and a ban on all demonstrations and even rallies. In the months that followed there were clashes between Asian and white youths in the Yorkshire town of Dewsbury and the West Bowling area of Bradford. The Rushdie issue was no longer a purely 'religious' one: there were long-term implications for community and race relations in a multi-ethnic British society.

3

The people of Britain may fairly be described as among the most patriotic in the world. Of all the nations, the British have indisputably shown the greatest attachment to their own customs and traditions over the past two or three centuries. As creators of the world's largest empire, the British do not take kindly to Muslim attempts to deviate from established British norms, especially when the Muslims have opted to settle in Britain.

Muslim citizens claim to be British as well as being Muslim. Implicit within the legislation and policy on multi-culturalism formulated since the mid 1960s has been the assumption that the identity of immigrants contains an amalgam of their own distinctive cultural heritage as well as the traditions of their chosen country of citizenship. This assumption has been widely questioned in the wake of the Rushdie affair. It has been the subject of a relatively dramatic recent declaration by the Tory Home Office minister John Patten—a theme to which we turn in the final section of this chapter. But it is wise to begin by exploring briefly issues clustered around the notion of a multi-cultural society accommodating opposed ideological convictions within a common liberal democratic framework.

During the Rushdie affair, newspapers with a pro-Conservative leaning have routinely declared that the myth of multi-culturalism has been exploded. Enoch Powell's allegedly prophetic warnings of inter-racial conflict have often been repeated in recent months. The immigrants must 'assimiliate'—accept the values of the host culture. Or else leave. There is a radical gulf, the contention continues, between Muslim aspiration and British political reality. There can be no question of Muslims being allowed to build a theocracy in the heart of Yorkshire. Barbara Amiel in *The Times* of 24 February 1989 speaks on behalf of many when she laments the presence of 'most intolerant segments of society' who wish to 'force their will over everyone else'. Amiel goes on to conclude that creating a multi-cultural society was itself a profound mistake.

Immediately one needs to be cautious. For the creation or destruction of a multi-cultural society is a subject that concerns not only Muslims. We have many brands of dissident opinion in contemporary Western society. There are Christians, Jews, secularists, Hindus, homosexuals, ordinary people concerned with the conservation of the environment and wild populations, Labour activists, animal rights campaigners, to mention just a few. The Rushdie affair may have served to endorse independently-founded scepticism about the very possibility of a multi-cultural society housing a Muslim minority. But one must not have illusions about the true scope of the scepticism. For even if the Muslim 'problem' (one thinks of the Nazis and the Final Solution) could be resolved, the issue of ideological division and conflict engendered by passionately held dissident opinion remains. That is a worry which is integral to liberal pluralistic society and must necessarily remain indefinitely on the agenda. Muslims or no Muslims, multi-culturalism is here to stay.

Once upon a time, in the heyday of multi-cultural rhetoric, Roy Jenkins and his disciples said that a multi-racial society not only tolerates diversity but encourages and welcomes it. That is much harder to believe these days. For those who have chosen to remain recognisably different, within the limits of the law, have suffered much indeed. The early immigrants accepted second-class status with a kind of resignation. These were men and women schooled in and comforted by the pious idioms of destiny and fate, never demanding the full rights of citizenship.

Their sons and daughters are different. They know their rights; and, paradoxically, the very society that has taught them the language of political demand and request has often denied them the rights they have asked for.

The problem arises when these confident British-born citizens wish to be both British and Muslim. Muslims want to integrate but not to assimilate: they want to compromise on matters of fashion but not of principle.

It is fair to say that a genuine pluralism in society can sometimes pose a threat to the dominion of beliefs and values that inform the common framework. Every society, including a multi-cultural one, is necessarily mono-cultural in its overall legal and political structure. The question is whether or not a variety of opposed ideological options can be fitted in, without friction, into the larger common framework. To Muslim eyes, in the post-Rushdie era, it looks as though Britain is at heart an essentially mono-cultural social structure with strongly liberal, secular, and nationalist foundations. To be sure, there is a pseudo-religious element in it too, for the established Anglican Church may equally be described as a religious or a secular (or semi-secular) institution. And though modern British society lives off the heritage of the Christian tradition, orthodox Christian doctrines hardly ever inform its political policy and indeed central Christian values of tolerance and charity are actually upheld by many liberals and secularists as well.

It cannot be surprising that such a society fails to attach any great importance to the religious outlook of Muslims. But given the presence of a sizeable Muslim community within Britain, Islam is no longer some exotic creed out there in the Middle East. Western society must allow political room for a faith that is wrongly seen as being too dogmatic and monolithic to fit into a pluralist culture. The problem of accommodation can only be solved if Westerners reject absurd propagandist portrayal of British Islam as a subversive force likely to destroy the fabric of multi-cultural and multi-lingual society. Over the Rushdie affair Muslims have merely asked for protection against gratuitous provocation, not for a licence to build a theocracy in Bradford.

The problem of peaceful co-existence of the Muslim minority with the white majority involves much more than the immediate issues spawned by the Rushdie tragedy. Take for example the controversial problem of 'separate' schooling for Muslim children. Muslims have been campaigning unsuccessfully for the right to establish their own voluntary-aided schools almost since the day they arrived in this country. Under the provisions of the 1944 Education Act, public and local authority funds are used to provide the running costs (and 85 per cent of the capital costs) of many Church of England, Roman Catholic and a few Jewish schools. Though Muslims are legally entitled to set up similar schools, their demands have been resolutely rejected by local and central government. There are many state schools, particularly in inner city areas of London, Bradford, Manchester, and Birmingham where pupils happen to be predominantly (or even almost entirely) Muslims. But, after almost two decades of lobbying MPs and Councillors, Muslims still do not have any voluntary-aided schools. In fact, several independent Muslim schools in Bradford, Dewsbury, and Blackburn funded by private donations, badly need to acquire voluntary-aided status in order to survive.

Both the left and the right reject Muslim demands. The argument from the left has generally been that all schooling with religious foundation is counter-productive in a multicultural society whose citizens aspire to live within a common, largely secular, framework of law. The Labour Party has always favoured changes in educational legislation which would make provision for Muslim needs within the mainstream and thus remove any basis for 'separatist' demands. The 1988 Education Reform Act reverses recent trends towards a multi-culturalism sensitive to minority needs by legislating for certain new specifically Christian attitudes and values within the so-called National Curriculum. The Muslim rejoinder to all this has been, quite rightly in my judgement, that as long as Jews and Christians have the legal right to operate voluntary-aided schools, it is wrong to prohibit Muslims from doing so. It may well be true that all such schooling is the remnant of a more religious age and should be replaced by a suitably modified mainstream state system appropriate to a secular society. But it is wholly indefensible to uphold inequality of treatment.

The arguments from the Conservative camp are much less convincing. The Muslim wish for voluntary-aided schools is interpreted by Conservatives as a wish for 'separate' identity, itself part of the larger desire for autonomy and cultural independence. And, as Douglas Hurd declared in his speech at the Birmingham Central Mosque in late February 1989, 'no community would thrive that withdrew itself from the mainstream of British life.' The Conservatives believe that Muslims want single sex provision, particularly for their daughters, because they fear that integration into British society involves too many compromises with Western decadence and neo-paganism. This demand for voluntary-aided schools is therefore seen as a demand for segregation — as a wish to create a cultural ghetto that is a bulwark against what are interpreted by Muslims as being the forces of secularity, sexual permissiveness and excessive materialism.

Many in Conservative as well as Labour circles think that giving Muslims the right to separate schools will cause harm to race relations as Muslims withdraw into their own cultural fortress. But race relations policy cannot properly be based on the assumption that Muslims should behave like white liberals. A truly pluralistic society can only be built on the premise that Muslims may, within certain specified legal limits, behave as Muslims. Ethnic minorities are entitled to resist the onslaught of English cultural imperialism. If we say that Indians and Pakistanis are only acceptable as members of the British community provided they integrate fully, then we are paying lip-service to the pluralist creed.

The political issues here run deep and the conceptual ones deeper still. Members of the ethnic minorities, particularly Muslims, need to examine carefully the proper limits of political demand in a multi-cultural society. This is a deeply involved issue for the Muslim conscience. We need to return to it in the final section. In this context, it is sufficient to record that Islam is a political faith that has internal resources for fiercely resisting any reduction into a piety in the private sector. Like all ideologies, Islam instinctively seeks the sanction of political power. Where Muslims live as minorities — as in Britain, India, and Israel — they effectively espouse a domesticated version of Islam. For, in general, secular Western democracies tolerate religious piety if and only if it is devoid of state sanction. To ask for a religious practice that enjoys the full support of political power is, in the final analysis, to ask for a theocracy.

There are issues of great immediacy here for the British government. What does one do with citizens who will not 'assimilate'? In a mature democracy, one cannot simply suppress them; nor can one properly accept every demand that they may make. Now Muslims constitute the largest religious community in Britain — for, strictly speaking, there are more practising (as opposed to merely professing) Muslims than Christians in modern Britain. Can it be fair to ignore the rights of such a group merely because its members look like foreigners?

4

'That Muslims are denied equal treatment under the law', said Roy Hattersley in a speech on 2 April 1989 at the Birmingham Central Mosque, 'is a matter of indisputable fact'. He is, of course, right. Settlers from Canada, New Zealand and Australia are welcome while those from India and Pakistan are merely immigrants who need to go through potentially racist testing procedures. Catholics and Jews have their own voluntary-aided schools reflecting their respective religious convictions while applications from Muslims are refused on the grounds that such schools are too 'separatist' in ethos. We need not extend this list in order to show that all races and religions do not receive equality of treatment in contemporary Britain.

There is, however, one particularly obvious inequality within the law which has been the subject of intense controversy during the Rushdie affair. Christian, or rather Anglican, sensibilities alone are officially protected. Anachronistic as it may appear in a largely secular society, blasphemy remains both a statutory and a common law offence in modern Britain. As the established church, the Church of England has, since the seventeenth century, uniquely enjoyed a legally enforceable protection against blasphemy (where the offence is orally published) and blasphemous libel (where it is published in a written form). Originally at least, any attack on the Anglican creed was necessarily an attack on the state. Blasphemy was therefore an indictable offence (triable by jury) of common law. It consisted of any publication of words attacking the Anglican denomination of the Christian faith or its scriptures in a manner so scurrilous as to pass beyond the limits of decent debate or controversy, and tending to lead to a breach of the peace. The offence is punishable by fine and imprisonment at the discretion of the court.

Britain is one of the few European countries in which the offence of blasphemy is still recognised in the legal system.

Despite consistent campaigns for its abolition for many decades—notably by The National Secular Society—the law of
blasphemy remains on the statute books. As late as 1979,
Mary Whitehouse was able to take *Gay News* to task, under
the blasphemy provisions, for publishing a poem in which
Christ experiences temptation to homosexuality. She won.
The House of Lords' decision in the case contained a slight
redefinition of the scope of the offence, in that blasphemous
libel is committed in any published writing concerning God
or Christ, the Christian religion, the Bible, or some sacred
subject, employing language that is scurrilous and abusive
and tending to vilify the Christian religion and hence having
a tendency to lead to a breach of the peace. In the case of
Whitehouse *v* Lemon and Gay News Limited, Lord Scarman
took the view that protection under the present legislation
does not extend beyond the Christian religion.

In 1981 the Law Commission published its Working Paper
no.79. The Commission provisionally proposed the abolition
without replacement of the common law offences of blasphemy and blasphemous libel on grounds of various short-
comings, including unclarity of the offence and its restriction
to Christianity. The Commission refused to propose a new
offence to deal with blasphemous conduct. To date, however,
the criminal law of blasphemy remains on the books; the Law
Commission's attempt to abolish it is one of several attempts
that have failed.

Muslim sensibilities are not protected in the United Kingdom under the current blasphemy law or indeed under any
contemporary enactment. *The Satanic Verses* does not seem
to contravene any contemporary British laws on race relations
or libel. To Muslims the fact that Rushdie has written vilely
enough to provoke anger but, as it happens, in a context that
enables him to avoid the normal penalty of law, is a sufficient
reason to suspect an inadequacy in the existing legislation.
Were Muhammad alive, he could of course successfully take
Rushdie and his publishers to court for blasphemous libel.
But there are no provisions for protecting the sensibilities of
individuals (or communities) whose self-esteem is linked to
their respect for Muhammad and his ideals.

The issue here is not merely of equality under the law. For one way, popular with secularists, of attaining equality of treatment would be simply to abolish the law of blasphemy. That would, however, be cold comfort to Muslims: while removing the privileged position afforded to a Christian denomination, it would leave Islam as unprotected as ever. Such a solution would rely on a drastic principle parallel in motivation to the impractical view that one way to solve all human problems is by exterminating the human race!

Although we can well understand why some Christians wish to preserve the blasphemy enactment in its current form, it is equally easy to sympathise with the Law Commission's recent recommendation of complete annulment. For the fact is, of course, that Britain is increasingly a *secular* liberal democracy in which Christian principles play a negligible role. It is true that some recent Conservative legislators are self-consciously concerned to make Christianity the faith of Britain; but that very attempt and the worry behind it betray the decline of Christian conviction. At any rate, the intellectual climate is hardly congenial to strident Muslim demands for an extension of the law in the wake of the Rushdie affair. Blasphemy—and related notions such as anathema and idolatry—are so remote from the daily concerns of most people in modern British society as to make their inclusion in legal restraint a thoroughly complicated affair. Indeed, blasphemy is a notion foreign even to many modern secularised Jews and Christians, let alone to secularists and other rejectors.

There are no doubt difficulties in extending the blasphemy law to protect the God of the Jews and Muslims as well as of the Christians. For one thing, under such a relatively comprehensive anti-blasphemy enactment, we could be sued for entertaining mutually contradictory beliefs. Muslims and Jews consider it blasphemous to declare that Jesus was God (or the Son of God). Yet it is clearly absurd to suggest that Jews and Muslims should sue the whole of Christendom for what is merely a standard belief. Christians, in turn, could accuse their religious cousins of blasphemy against God in denying his incarnation in Christ. And there are other problems too. We cannot simply ignore the religious sensibilities of Hindus who wish to protect a whole pantheon of deities. Yet the normal Hindu's polytheistic belief is anathema to Jews, Christians and Muslims alike. An even-handed and fair blasphemy law is undeniably difficult to formulate even if we assume — as perhaps we shouldn't — that atheistic humanist traditions do not deserve legal protection.

If we refuse to extend the blasphemy provisions, the refusal must be for the right reasons. Neither inability to define blasphemy nor the presence of agreed difficulties in application of the proposed law is a sufficient reason for refusal to legislate in this area of sensibility. Virtually all areas of profound human concern are the subject of keen disagreement, but that fact alone does not deter us from making laws to regulate behaviour. There are arguments, sometimes intractable, about the precise definition of many offences; public and parliamentary debate can, however, jointly sort out the details once the underlying principles have been accepted. The fact that we cannot provide an uncontroversial definition of an offence can never be an adequate ground for abandoning the search for formulating proper legal restraint and the corresponding punishment.

It is important to know the purpose of law. Legislation cannot make us fully tolerant of one another. Those who hate Islam will, even under a tighter law, seek other means of abusing it. But the ability of human beings to evade even the most precise legal regulation is no reason for refusing to impose legal constraint. 'Law does not', in Martin Luther King's famous remark, 'change the heart — but it does restrain the heartless'. And that is already a great achievement.

Nor will it do to entrust matters to the discretion of individuals in the hope that men and women can never be utterly insensitive to each other's feelings. Arguments in favour of self-censorship are, in political and ideological contexts, weak and implausible. It is unsurprising that we do not merely request racists to self-censor their literature. The law does it for them since the issue is too public in its consequences to be left purely to private decision and discretion. There is no evidence, historically or contemporaneously, for the view that human beings will cease to harm the interests of others once the fetters of law are removed to make room for voluntary charity.

The law may be a blunt instrument but we cannot do without it. In the context of the Rushdie affair there is an urgent need for an enactment to protect Muslim sensibilities against gratuitous provocation. Whether or not the enactment involves an extension of the existing blasphemy regulations is really a matter of detail. It may well be that, in a secular society like Britain, the Muslim's best bet is to campaign for a law making certain kinds of conduct or publication socially unacceptable as opposed to religiously offensive. Lord Jakobovits, the Chief Rabbi, has wisely counselled Muslims along these lines, arguing that some enactment should prohibit 'socially intolerable conduct calculated or likely to incite revulsion or violence by holding up religious beliefs to scurrilous contempt . . . ' (*The Times*, 4 March 1989). Thus, for example, Muslims may contend that while insulting a revered but dead religious leader like Muhammad need not be an indictable offence in a secular society, such polemic could excite the anger of those citizens whose self-image is created by reference to his ideals and lifestyle—and hence may lead to a breach of the peace. In short, some writing may defame an entire community.

The Commission for Racial Equality has not established that Muslims are a discrete group of people bound together by a common faith. The Race Relations Act does not, except in Ulster, identify religion as a ground for discrimination; accordingly the equal opportunities policies of local authorities do not normally interpret it as a relevant determinant in service delivery. Yet, in the case of Muslims, the Rushdie saga has strongly indicated that religious affiliation is far more central than colour and ethnic origin in determining the needs and aspirations of Muslims. Indeed, for Muslims, faith takes on a significance at least as great as race and gender in any proper interpretation of their self-identity. The demands of Muslim communities cannot always be subsumed under the geographical category of Asian. In fact, Asians often see themselves as religious groups, i.e. as Sikhs, Hindus, and Muslims. It is entirely reasonable to identify Muslims as a distinct group of people on grounds of their self-professed Islamic identity.

In the wake of the Rushdie debate, the Race Relations Act needs amendment. Ethnicity cannot be the sole factor in identifying a group as a community with shared convictions. The Commission for Racial Equality has rightly viewed with sympathy attempts to classify Jews and Travellers as distinct groups. Why not Muslims? Unfortunately, the Commission is largely secular in its guiding principles; most of the architects of race relations policies are secularists eager to deny the importance of religious allegiance as a factor in human social identity.

5

The Rushdie affair has not yet been resolved. It may never be resolved to the satisfaction of all concerned parties. After Khomeini's *fatwa* in February 1989 it became rapidly clear that both Rushdie's supporters and his detractors were getting ready for a long night. We had a radical disagreement on our hands.

Do we? I believe that the Rushdie controversy is not intractable. To show that it is incapable of rational resolution would be effectively fatal to the Muslim case. It is clearly in the interests of the liberal and non-Muslim constituency to pretend that Islamic demands concerning Rushdie's book are unacceptably foreign to the spirit of Western democracy. But are these demands, properly assessed, incapable of being met? Does the debate over *The Satanic Verses* ultimately involve a principle concerning which Muslims radically disagree with their opponents? Or is the dispute resolvable on the basis of empirically obtainable evidence about the harm, socially and individually, certain publications may cause?

The central difficulty here is prejudicial rigour. If only non-Muslims would assess the Muslim case on the basis of evidence rather than on the basis of negative views formed independently of the relevant evidence. The objectivity and restraint that Western commentators loudly proclaim have completely deserted them during the Rushdie affair, whatever may be said of their assessment of other non-Islamic issues.

Let us suppose, for the sake of argument, that someone had published a novel praising a character recognisably Hitlerian, with scenes as offensive to Jews as those in *The Satanic Verses* are to Muslims. Would we allow, let alone passionately patronise, such a publication? Should we? In 1987 the management of London's Royal Court Theatre abandoned its plans for staging Jim Allen's play *Perdition*, which questioned the received account of the Holocaust. Influential Jews stopped the production, though without enlisting the powers of the state or requesting supplementary legislation. The management conceded that the play would distress Jews. Yet the same theatre staged the play *Iranian Nights* by Tariq Ali and Howard Brenton, at the height of the Rushdie affair, despite protests from Muslims who argued that it trivialised Islamic ideals. Presumably, Jews are much more easily outraged than Muslims.

Fortunately, Jewish suffering has a special place in Western eyes. As a community that threw in its lot with the Christian West it has for long been subject to focussed brutality. Yet, in many ways, the decrease in Western hatred of Jewish communities has, sadly, gone hand-in-hand with a proportionate increase in hatred of Muslim communities. It were as though the Western mind must feed on resentment towards at least one community at any given time. It happens to be Muslims now—the new Jews of contemporary Western society. How else can one explain the sheer depth of Western anger at the Muslim decision to defend Islamic ideals in the face of an intolerable provocation?

To accuse contemporary Western commentators and politicians of prejudice and unfair attitudes is not to suggest that things cannot change for the better. After all, unlike the Jews, Muslims have lived in Britain only for a few decades. It is unrealistic to expect them to attain to positions of power and prestige overnight. But it is important not to entrust an unjust state of affairs only to patience and the future. There is work to be done in the present.

More or less all Western democracies have reacted in one

way or another to the Rushdie affair, especially after hearing Khomeini's edict. The French authorities have whole-heartedly condemned Khomeini's *fatwa* and threatened to prosecute any Muslim in France who openly avows support for it. There has been no corresponding condemnation of Rushdie, even for bad taste. The Americans have also come down heavily on the Muslims for their opposition to Rushdie, without any corresponding judgement about the possible propriety of Muslim indignation. Of all the Western governments, Britain alone has reacted cautiously and sympathetically. While condemning Khomeini's verdict, there has also been some sympathy for Muslim alienation and anguish. Thus, for example, even the most dedicated Muslim campaigners have not been threatened with deportation; indeed even those openly calling for Rushdie's death have been tolerated.

Muslims have been deeply frustrated by the inaction of the British government, by what Muslims have perceived to be the slow rate of democratic reform. Comparisons with the Chinese government's fast ban on the work of 'the Chinese Rushdie' have often been made. In March 1989 a Shanghai publishing house issued a book entitled *Sexual Customs*. It was put forward as a sociological survey of sexual mores world-wide. The authors, Ke Le and Sang Ya, argued preposterously that minarets were phallic symbols, the domes of mosques represented female breasts and that the believers' main purpose in going on the annual pilgrimage to Mecca was to commit bestiality with camels. There were demonstrations by outraged Muslims; the book was immediately banned on the grounds that it had intolerably provoked a religious minority.

Yet the temptation to denounce the British democratic process by comparison is to be staunchly resisted. Mature democracies can indeed be frustratingly slow in responding to the perceived needs of citizens; the tempo of democratic change certainly angers and frustrates. But while a Communist political order may react immediately, such action can have far more tragic results. The massacre at Tianamen Square in 1989 is fortunately no part of democracy. Inaction is surely better than widespread and hasty suppression of the rights of citizens.

6

'Submit to the will of your God, by all means; but submit to British law first'. An original definition of Islam has been proffered by commentators and politicians as Muslims have refused to wind down their protest against Rushdie's book. There has been no shortage of threats or analyses from the authorities—and it is not always easy to tell the two apart.

Listening to Conservatives like Douglas Hurd and Kenneth Baker, one might be excused for thinking that Islam is the white man's latest burden. One can certainly detect a residue of colonial arrogance in some of the comments made by British politicians in recent months. Westerners are once again taking upon themselves the morally demanding task of civilising backward Muslim people suddenly re-emerging with renewed confidence as a result of recently acquired wealth.

The most influential declaration has come from John Patten, the Home Office Minister of State responsible for race relations. On 4 July 1989, he published an open letter to a number of Muslim leaders rejecting their demands for a state ban on Rushdie's book and reminding them of their obligation to live harmoniously in a multi-cultural British society. Two weeks later, in a letter addressed to, among others, the Chairman of the Commission for Racial Equality, Patten argued that being British imposed on Muslims (and other communities) a duty to respect British laws. He warned Muslims against making unacceptable demands as citizens of a kingdom that was not Islamic in its constitution. He concluded that British Muslims should not cultivate dual loyalties where one of them conflicts with the obligations entailed by British citizenship.

Patten's 'On Being British', as it is called, raises many large questions in the debate about multi-culturalism, cultural purity and identity. It comes, oddly enough, at a time when British identity is likely to be diluted (if not contaminated) by Britain's membership of the EEC and the effects of the

European community's legislation for 1992. (Many individuals in Britain already enjoy dual citizenship.) We cannot here explore the many implications of Patten's position. Directly with respect to Muslims, Patten's declaration raises several obvious questions. Is the ideal of multi-culturalism now being effectively abandoned? How will Muslims choose if faced with the choice between being British and being Muslim?

Patten seems to be favouring the melting-pot model, popular with some multi-culturalists, rather than the model put forward by Roy Jenkins in 1966 when he called for equal opportunities for ethnic minorities in an atmosphere of cultural diversity sustained by mutual tolerance. The present Conservative government may well favour assimilation in the light of recent developments that seem to suggest a Muslim desire for cultural separatism. Certainly, some Muslim organisations have demanded a recognition of Islamic family law for British Muslims—with an implied call for the legalisation of polygamy. There have even been some extravagant comments about a whole Islamic charter for British society. It is not difficult to see why some Tory commentators have cautioned Muslims against asking for a miniature theocracy within the United Kingdom.

Though multi-culturalism is not an invention of modern Britain, British society has recently been engaged in a pioneering experiment in creating multi-ethnic social harmony. It would be unfair to dismiss its fruits and successes merely because we have come up with an obstacle. But the Rushdie affair will certainly provide a crucial experiment for the multi-cultural ideal in liberal democracy. The resolution of the issue will interest Muslims who themselves have in the past created a civilisation that patronised multi-cultural and multi-religious ambitions.

Multi-cultural ideals are visibly strained when citizens are actually offered a choice between two opposed identities. Patten's warning to the Muslims points to the necessary tension between loyalty to the state of one's chosen country of citizenship, on the one hand, and an allegiance to a larger religious community that transcends national boundaries, on

127

the other. British Muslims are citizens of the United Kingdom; but they are equally members of a global Islamic community. In this they are no different from Catholics and Jews who are citizens of a given nation but retain some loyalty to their larger ethnic or religious fellowship. There are duties to both; the conflicts that are created usually remain indefinitely on the agenda of loyalties. Normally Muslims are asked to compromise routinely on matters of taste or fashion—but not on matters of principle. There is rarely the need for a painful choice between two opposed allegiances both based on fundamental principle. But where circumstances force such a choice, no authentic Muslim can hesitate about which loyalty comes first.

Epilogue: The Summer of Discontent

1

I have a right to truth, and to publish truth, let society suffer or not suffer by it. That society which suffers by truth should be otherwise constituted.

The writer of these uncompromising words is not Salman Rushdie. The words are in fact penned by the seventeenth-century militant rationalist William Hammon. Yet, for all the cultural and historical discrepancy between the two writers, the quoted creed may well serve to introduce the controversy over *The Satanic Verses*.

'I have a right to publish the *truth*', says the courageous author. By all means. But could Rushdie say the same in defence of his book? To be sure, someone might retort, the question of truth or falsity cannot properly arise at all: *The Satanic Verses* is proffered as a fictional account. But, as we saw in chapter 2, it remains too close to actual Islamic history for Rushdie's claim to be convincing.

The issue remains. A right to publish unpalatable truth and indeed criticism is surely not equivalent to a right to publish propaganda and abuse. For all the apparent simplicity of this distinction, it is a distinction that remains important and unambiguous. Its exact formulation and application are centrally relevant to any intellectual resolution of the Rushdie controversy.

'I have a right to truth', Rushdie may well have said. And indeed he has every right to teach the Muslims some truths about themselves. Perhaps Islam needs a major heretical movement that could jolt Muslims out of their complacency and persuade them to take seriously the many challenges of secular modernity. But such a movement must be recognisably Islamic. Otherwise Muslims will merely either ignore it

129

or condemn it. Rushdie is too abrupt, too eager to rupture all links with the Islamic context that might guide Muslims into making appropriate concessions to modern thought. The temper of revolutionary proposals is no less significant than their content. Even if a Rushdie-like mood—aristocratic and supercilious—may occasionally be necessary in the face of entrenched orthodoxy, the content of iconoclastic proposals need not lapse into abuse.

But what's wrong with abuse? Don't we often rely on satire and comic hyperbole to make valid points? How else can one cut the gods down to size? I gave a relatively detailed response to this and similar retorts in chapter 2. Suffice it to say here that there are many techniques of reverent yet penetrating scepticism that do not carry the dangers attending satire and ridicule. It is unwise for us in a multi-cultural society to encourage a form of denigration and abuse which can breed resentment to the point of strife and public disorder. It is one thing to say that the Islamic tradition should, like all others, co-exist with a contemporary habit of mind which interrogates and questions even cherished convictions. It is quite another to argue that Muslims, or indeed non-Muslims, should tolerate wanton prejudice or otherwise propagandist material published under the pretext of criticism.

2

By a complex process of events, the defence of Salman Rushdie and his novel has, mistakenly, become a defence of Western values. The scenario is certainly stranger than fiction: a virulently anti-Islamic book is written by an Indian apostate living in Britain, and an Iranian cleric orders his execution. The oddity of the tale doesn't end here. Mrs Thatcher's government, condemned as racist by the author, leaps to his defence. The Islamic world and the Western world become ideologically polarised almost overnight.

What precisely are the Western values that the defenders of Rushdie are upholding? And why are they prepared to pay such a high price for upholding them? It is too late in the night for anyone, Muslim or non-Muslim, to pretend that freedom of speech (or conscience) is the central value being defended here. That particular right of democratic society is always exercised with due restraint; any society in which freedom of speech were absolute would probably cease to be a society at all. Though many defenders of freedom have recently spoken in tones high and holy, it is difficult to take them seriously in view of the double, even triple moral standards they regularly employ. Occasionally, freedom of speech may well be absolute and exercised with impunity—but only at the expense of powerless groups.

What, then, is the real reason for the universal and indeed spontaneous outrage in the Western constituency? It seems to me that the Muslim response over the Rushdie affair challenges the cultural imperialism implicit in the occidental outlook. Why should the West dictate the mental and moral fashion for the rest of the civilised world? Only Muslims have dared to ask that question. For to ask such a question is already to betray mental independence.

The fact is of course that there exists a small clique of ideologues, with privileged access to publishing houses and newspaper columns, who have become the self-appointed priests of the cult of 'democratic' freedom. For these individuals, the defence of Rushdie is actually a form of self-defence—an attempt to preserve a value system based on the exploitation of the weaknesses of unprotected minorities entertaining radically different moral or religious convictions.

The Rushdie affair is, in effect, part of an ideological battle between Islam and the West. There can be no other explanation for the sheer bitterness and lengthiness of a campaign that started off as a request, surely modest enough, for the removal from circulation of one gratuitously provocative and relatively inferior piece of literature.

3

'A free society is one', it has been said, 'in which it is safe to be unpopular.' On such a definition, Britain may not, in the aftermath of the Rushdie provocation, remain a free society— at least for Muslims. It has never been entirely safe to be a Muslim here; but, particularly in cities with large Asian populations, the local authorities have over the past decades made genuine and partly successful attempts to combat racism and inequality of opportunity. Unfortunately, the fruits of that labour have vanished overnight. Muslims are now being singled out for prejudicial treatment. The old racism against all blacks is more focussed now. Even before the Rushdie episode began, Muslims were systematically victimised and harassed because of their conspicuous refusal to 'integrate'. To be sure, Muslims were making all the concessions required by law: but nothing more. Much more than other minority groups, Muslims wanted to retain their own faithful heritage as well as reap the benefits of British citizenship. It was necessarily an uneasy alliance; Rushdie has made it a virtually impossible one.

The events surrounding the publication of *The Satanic Verses* have long-term consequences for the sizeable Muslim community now settled in the United Kingdom. In the short term, there will be increased discrimination by white employers against members of a community already disproportionately affected by economic recession. There will be an increase in the discrimination against Muslim students and teachers in intellectual life—though that is not excessively worrying since such discrimination has always been at virtually peak levels. In the long term, the consequences could be either devastating or beneficial depending on the government's reaction. If the current level of resentment and anger is allowed to increase, then Muslims will suffer severe deprivation as the white majority engages in systematic oppression of 'these barbarians'. If the government intervenes, establishes a dialogue with their Muslim citizens, the affair could end on a constructive note.

At the height of the Rushdie affair I wrote in the *Guardian* that the next time there are gas chambers in Europe, there is little doubt concerning who will be inside them. If we make allowances for the shock tactics and overlook the hyperbole in a journalistic piece written after all in the heat of the moment, the remark is not entirely without point. If society deteriorates—as societies can—there will be dire consequences for the defenceless Muslims. Indeed there has recently been a revival of Fascism in Britain, France, Germany and other European countries. The vocabulary of the Final Solution is not necessarily confined to the Germany of the Third Reich and the Jews. And who would have thought that a society which had historically produced great philosophers and musicians could go down in an orgy of violence and anger? The nasty side of human nature is never too far below the surface of civilised existence.

The Muslims will not be alone in their suffering. As a result of the Rushdie affair, the lives of Western hostages held in the Lebanon have been further endangered. More broadly, given the volatile ideological climate in the Muslim world, it is safe to predict an increase in political terrorism in the coming decade. The targets will include British citizens seen as conspirators against Islam and the Muslims. Travelling these days is hazardous enough without the additional risks that political entanglement brings.

4

Though global in its implications, the Rushdie saga is essentially a British one. It started in Britain; in some sense, it needs to end there too.

The manner in which the Anglo-Rushdie affair terminates will be of great political significance. For it will determine whether or not Britain, as a potentially mature democracy, can accord to all citizens a right to equal and just treatment. Unless the authorities wish to suppress their Muslim citizens, they can no longer ignore Muslim demands for the enactment of legislation protecting Islamic sensibilities.

To enact laws to protect the deepest feelings of Muslims is not to 'give in' to that old Iranian cleric Ayatollah Khomeini. Well before the Iranian edict was promulgated, domestic Muslim populations in Britain's metropolitan cities had been campaigning for the withdrawal of *The Satanic Verses*. Subsequent events have, sadly, created a deadlock in which both parties see victory as a matter of honour. Yet justice is what the Muslims seek; victory at all costs is not an Islamic doctrine. At any rate, as long as injustice prevails, we are all losers. It is a false triumphalism that wishes to defeat Muslims in order that society may win.

It is high time for the age-old veto on any sympathetic assessment of Muslim aspirations, initially imposed during the Crusades, to be lifted and for Muslims to be given a fair hearing in the corridors of power. Otherwise they will remain alienated and isolated second-class citizens faced increasingly with the threat of organised racism. Even if the goal of providing equality of opportunity and just treatment is a long-term one, Parliament needs to enact laws immediately to protect Muslims against gratuitous provocation. It does not greatly matter how this protection is achieved: by an extension of the scope of the law against blasphemy or by amending the public order Act or the criminal libel Act or indeed by any other appropriate enactment. These are details to be sorted out by public and parliamentary debate. But the underlying principle needs immediate recognition in the wake of the Anglo-Rushdie episode.

It is in the interests of the establishment to pretend that the Rushdie affair will die a natural death. But this is a mistaken diagnosis if only because it will still leave a permanent scar. Words can hurt; and there are wounds time cannot heal.

5

While the Liberal Inquisition was at its height, many Muslims advised each other in a moment of despair, to be patient and steadfast. Some were tempted to entrust the whole matter to patience, prayer and the future. They recognised, rightly, that there are no short-cuts to victory in matters of the faith. And even when achieved, it is only the wise who recognise it. But many Muslims inferred, wrongly, that patience and prayer are substitutes for active struggle and militant witness.

The campaign has not been without success for the Muslims. As a group, they have shown the liberal establishment that faith can, and sometimes needs to, move mountains,

even in a secular country. Many points have been made—
and made with a passion and enthusiasm alien to the West in
matters of religion. No sincere observer of the campaign
against the book can remain unimpressed by the moral integrity of the Muslim motivation.

But the rewards are much larger. Though there is a paradox
of publicity—many more will read the book, given the fuss we
have made—Rushdie's message has been pre-empted. Many
individuals will continue to buy the book out of motives of
curiosity, or, in some cases, malice. But no one, Muslim or
non-Muslim, can read *The Satanic Verses* with the degree of
ignorance and innocence required for the poison to be effec-
tive. It is now widely if secretly recognised that Rushdie's
book was written for instant fame and easy money. And, in
any case, whether people read it or not, Muslims have shown
that a society should not, as a matter of principle, patronise
its publication.

On every score of political expediency it may have been
wiser never to have started a fight with such powerful enemies. At any rate, it is certainly dangerous to refuse to drop
the issue at this stage. But Muslims see it as a matter of
principle—and considerations of expediency and danger can
have little or no relevance in such affairs.

What remain in our thoughts, for a quiet evening, are
myriad variations on an influential slogan about power and
powerlessness—all equally trivial, all equally true or equally
false depending on one's mood. The pen is mightier than the
sword; the sword is mightier than the pen; the pen is useless
without the sword; the pen is mightiest with the sword. It has
taken Islam to remind us that faith should be mightier than
both.

Certainly, the sword is useless without the pen. Even if the
British government and people score a victory over their
Muslim citizens, through threats or the use of naked force,
the moral victory belongs to those who stand up for what
is right and just, not fearing the reproach of the powerful
but unjust. It is here that faith properly tests and tries men
and women. Faith is as faith does—in the hour of trial. The

Be Careful with Muhammad!

human task, the human obligation, is to plead for and, if
necessary, fight for what is right and just. Victory is, for the
Muslim conscience, by the grace of God—our Lord and their
Lord.

136